# A Handbook
## for
## *Adjunct & Part-Time*
## Faculty & Teachers
## of Adults

Donald Greive

*Fourth Edition*

*To Order, contact:*

**The Adjunct Advocate**
P.O. Box 130117
Ann Arbor, MI 48113-0117
1(734)930-6854
FAX: 1(208)728-3033

First printing:  May, 2001

© *2003 The Adjunct Advocate, Inc.*

**Library of Congress Data**
Catalog Card Number:

ISBN: 0-940017-28-8 (paperback)
ISBN: 0-940017-29-6 (hardcover)

Printed in the United States of America

# Table of Contents

# Table of Figures

## Acknowledgments

A major revision of a publication such as this depends upon the contributions and support of many individuals. Although it is not possible to recognize all, some are of such importance as to deserve special mention.

First and foremost, I am indebted to Catherine Worden who stepped forward to assume the role of editor and publisher in bringing the book not only to its proper structure but also in carrying out the many details necessary for its successful printing and publication. Her contributions were essential to "making it happen." We are indebted to Peggy Nesbit for editing and proofreading, as well as for the page-layout, and to Brian Sooy & Co. for the cover design.

We are especially appreciative of the contributions of those professionals who use the *Handbook* for their completion of the surveys and their suggestions. Those suggestions contributed greatly to the changes in content to enhance and improve the book.

Of special note is the contribution of Gary Wheeler, whose knowledge and ability to put into words the impact of technology is a major contribution. Finally, and of equal importance, are the contributions of Janet Greive for her efforts in preparing the manuscript. To these individuals and all all others whose suggestions were incorporated, I am forever grateful.

*Don Greive*

## Preface to the Fourth Edition

It has been over a decade since *A Handbook for Adjunct/Part-time Faculty and Teachers of Adults* was first published with the intention of supporting adjunct faculty in their teaching role. In that time the book has reached hundreds of colleges and universities and thousands of adjunct faculty throughout the U.S. and Canada. In recent years, however, the mission of higher education instruction has shifted to a greater emphasis upon student-centered learning and the utilization of technology. This revision of the *Handbook* attempts to recognize that shift and provide adjunct and part-time faculty with the contemporary tools necessary for successful classroom instruction.

I believe that we have accomplished that goal in this revision without sacrificing the fundamental strengths of the original publication, i.e. emphasizing instructor-proven techniques and strategies for teaching. The use of adjuncts continues to increase, however, and the fundamental problems remain… most adjunct faculty still maintain full-time jobs outside the institution and have limited time available for extensive reading and research concerning teaching. This publication is designed to accommodate that situation by providing faculty with brief and enlightening information, available at their fingertips for easy reference, presented in a practical informative format.

*Don Greive*

## *How To Get the Most Out of This Book...*

One of the major changes in the new edition of this handbook is the use of icons to highlight important information for the reader.

**Keys to Success:** Wheneve you see this icon, you'll want to take special note because these are tried and true tips to improve your classroom performance.

**Caution Light:** Whenever you see this icon, you'll know that other successful adjunct and part-time instructors have discovered what NOT to do while teaching.

In addition to the icons, an index has been compiled for ease of use. As with the previous edition, the table of contents has remained very detailed to get you to the topic that most interests you at the moment.

So you can read this handbook from front to back or keep it handy as a quick reference on many of the most important areas of concern for new and experienced adjunct and part-time faculty.

---

This is your quick reference for good teaching. You may use this book as a manual, a guide, or for professional reading. It contains practical and informative tips to assist you with your instructional tasks. It is written in a user-friendly manner for your convenience. Enjoy it and GOOD TEACHING.

---

# CHAPTER 1
## TEACHING: WHAT'S IT ALL ABOUT

### Orientation to College and Adult Teaching

In the coming decades, teachers of college and adult students will be faced with many challenges that did not previously exist. Compared to the classroom of former years, the evolution to the modern classroom has caused significant changes. The influx of multicultural and multilingual students, the impact of technology, and the admission of students with differing academic preparation have demanded the attention of educators everywhere. In addition, changing economic and political pressures throughout the world have impacted education and, you, the instructor.

You will feel the impact whether you teach in a continuing education program for business/industry or the military; in a liberal arts college with time-honored traditions and values; in a community college with an open door policy; in a public research university with postgraduate programs; or in an adult education center. The students of today will be more highly motivated, more challenging and in many ways more enjoyable to teach.

With the concern for accountability and the realization that there are established strategies and techniques for instruction, there is greater emphasis upon quality instruction. Adult students employed in business and industry expect a planned and organized classroom. It is no longer a question of whether there are going to be instructional objectives and strategies for teaching; it is a question of how skilled instructors are in developing and delivering them.

One of the most important factors, however, remains the human element of teaching. If you enjoy being a teacher, there is nothing wrong with telling the students that you are there because you enjoy teaching. Being cheerful, open, and understanding is always an asset to good teaching. Students will like to hear your experiential anecdotes — share them. Look upon the class as a project. Adult students expect planning and preparation and will not rebel if it is required. Be aware of your cultural and intellectual environment. Strive to be a good and successful instructor and your teaching experiences will be exciting, rewarding, and satisfying.

It might help you to take a few moments before your first class to meditate about your reasons for teaching. This will do two things: it will encourage you to more clearly identify your personal goals and it will increase your confidence.

There may be students who question why someone with your expertise would spend their time teaching a college course. Be prepared. Have a few answers ready if students ask. If they don't ask, you might want to include it in your personal introduction. You certainly have good reasons. It might be to your advantage to communicate them. You may just enjoy teaching, like interaction with others, like the stimulation, enjoy being in front of a group, or feel it improves your own skills.

You should also give thought to your role in your institution. In short "what is an adjunct/part-time instructor?" Too often adjunct faculty, and thus their students, feel their place within the institution is a temporary and unimportant one. Nothing could be farther from the truth. Adjunct faculty in recent years have assumed a greater responsibility to the educational mission of their colleges and universities. Many institutions depend upon adjunct faculty for 50 percent or more of credit hours of instruction taught. Also in many institutions, adjunct and part-time faculty serve on committees and accept other non-instructional assignments. Finally, adjunct faculty often teach in specialized areas where specific qualifications and expertise is needed. Yes, whether you are a continuing adjunct or a last-minute part-time replacement, yours is an important role and necessary to the integrity and success of your institution.

 As with their full-time colleagues, teaching is still a vocation for many adjunct instructors, a calling to those individuals who enjoy being with people and feel an intrinsic satisfaction in helping others to grow.

In your role as an adjunct/part-time instructor, you will realize many of the intrinsic rewards of the profession. You are repaying your profession for its contributions to your own personal and professional development. There is satisfaction in providing service to your community and you will find that teaching builds self esteem, offers personal rewards, and keeps you intellectually alive. Teaching can provide intellectual growth, community recognition and respect, and the development of new professional contacts. The satisfactions and rewards of being a good adjunct instructor are real and many.

## Establishing a Teaching Environment

Over the past two decades, there has been a major movement in higher education called "the learning college" movement or community-centered learning. Quite simply, this means that learning has become student-centered rather than instructor-centered. This is especially important to adjunct faculty members, most of whom come from the surrounding community and thus are aware of community mores.

When establishing a student-centered learning environment, one should first examine the teacher-student relationship. The simple and most obvious way to develop a relationship with your students is be yourself and be honest, establishing communication in the classroom the same as you would in any other human endeavor. There are, however, additional specific steps that can be taken to establish a proper learning environment. Helen Burnstad describes four areas in which the learning environment should be examined: teacher expectations, teaching behavior, physical space, and strategies for creating an environment for learning (Burnstad, 2000). Although it is impossible to describe these areas completely in this handbook, some of Burnstad's major points are examined below:

- *Teacher expectations.* It is important first, that each instructor have a clear picture of his or her own style and expectations. The expectations that you as an instructor have of yourself may differ considerably from those of the students in your class. This does not mean that you need to change your style. However, you need to examine the expectations of your students in terms of their position (rather than your position) on issues and principles that may arise in class. Also it is important that you consider your own teaching goals. From this you can frame your philosophy and intent regarding the content of the course.

- *Teacher behaviors.* It is important that you examine your presence in the classroom. Students will sense whether you really love your subject matter or are teaching the course to reach some unrelated professional goal. A pleasant personality is important. Enthusiasm may be demonstrated through energy and engaging in activities with students. Remember, your feelings concerning the expectations of your students will unwittingly be reflected in the success or failure of your students.

- *Physical space.* Although in most cases you will have little control over the physical aspects of the classroom environment, there are several things that can be done by the instructor. If possible, you may physically move seats so that dialogue and eye contact are easier. You should monitor the attention span of your students; sense the need for reinforcement; calculate the time-on-task; and encourage students to move, interact and ask questions.

- *Environmental Strategies.* Some strategies that can improve the classroom environment include:

1. **Introducing yourself** to your students with some personal anecdotes.

2. **Being prepared** for students with diverse backgrounds.

3. **Using an activity for getting to know** your students, whether a game, a writing assignment, or reference card, etc.

4. **Learning each student's name** and providing ways for students to get to know one another.

5. **Preparing a complete and lively syllabus.** You can have your students from a previous class leave a legacy by asking them to write a letter for incoming students then sharing it.

6. **Using classroom assessment** techniques.

Finally, whether one is establishing a classroom environment or doing day-to-day activities, it is important that you be as positive in your student-teacher relationships as toward your subject matter. Make yourself available for student contact, either personally or electronically. Take a personal interest in each student and never judge or stereotype students.

## Characteristics of Good Teaching

Using one's mind in the pursuit of knowledge and at the same time sharing it with others is very gratifying. The responsibility for a class and the potential influence on students can be very stimulating. It remains stimulating, however, only so long as the instructor continues to grow and remains dynamic.

The qualities of good teaching are quite simple:

- Know your subject content.

- Know and like your students.

- Understand our culture.

- Possess professional teaching skills and strategies.

Knowing your subject means simply that you have a command of your discipline and the capability of calling upon resources. Knowing students is part of the teaching process and is aided by formal and informal communication within and outside the classroom. Understanding our cultural milieu has become increasingly complex for todays' instructor. Sensitivity to the diverse cultures in your classroom is necessary to succeed in teaching. Finally, it is necessary that you continue to develop and improve strategies and techniques for the delivery of instruction in the classroom.

Some characteristics that students look for in good teachers are:

- Being knowledgeable, organized, and in control.

- Getting students actively involved in their learning.

- Helping students understand the course objectives and goals.

- Being a facilitator, not a director.

- Knowing the latest trends and technology.

- Stimulating discussion utilizing ice breakers.

- Preparing professional materials and handouts.

### The First Class

No matter how long you have been teaching you will always be faced with the another "first class." If it is your very first time teaching as an adjunct, the strategies you incorporate are not significantly different from those used on the first class of any future course you may teach. There will always be anxieties and some nervousness before the first class. For experienced faculty who have just completed a course where rapport and communication had been developed, you now face a new class where your students are strangers to you and you are a stranger to them. The anxieties of this returning class are the same as those of the very first class that you will or have ever taught. It is often stated that you never get the second chance to make a first impression and this is certainly true in the world of teaching.

 In preparing for the first class, keep in mind that it is nearly impossible to anticipate all situations. The speed at which your first class presentation goes will vary from class to class. Many times student response is significantly greater or less than expected. Having excessive material prepared for the first class will allay this problem and is worth the extra effort in confidence gained.

Another stress reliever when facing your first class is knowing yourself as a teacher. Anyone mature enough to be teaching has some feeling of his or her own personal characteristics. Most of us are average in appearance; however, we usually have gone through life compensating for our variations from the average. There is no more need to be self-conscious in front of a class than there is in any social situation. However, minor compensations may help. If you have a tendency toward casual or even sloppy appearance, appearing neat and professional will pay off. If you have a light voice, practice in expression may be well worth the time spent. Generally speaking, students' first impression of you will include your appearance and actions. If you are timid — take charge. Being in control pays off not only in eliminating barriers to classroom communication, but in developing self-confidence in teaching.

Since the first class is a form of a social introduction, it will influence all successive meetings. You should have a detailed plan for the first class period which will diminish the threats and anxieties of expecting the unexpected. It might be helpful to speak with other teachers who have taught the class in an attempt to anticipate students' questions or concerns. It is a good idea to physically visit the classroom where you will be teaching before the first day. If possible, find out who your students are, their ages, their background, and any previous courses or prerequisites they may have taken.

Listed below are some suggestions that will help alleviate any anxieties and get your class off to a good start:

- **Plan an activity** that allows students to get involved immediately. It may simply be an information-gathering exercise.

- **Initiate casual conversation** with and among the students prior to presenting the specifics of the course.

- **Share anecdotes.** Students are interested in your background and some of your course-related experiences.

- **Introduce the following items** to your students: the name and number of the course, the objectives of the course, the text(s), syllabus, the dates of all exams, and your grading system. Finally take a roll call to establish that everyone there intends to be in your class.

- **Make certain you are early**, at least 20 minutes before the start of the first class. If possible, greet your students as they come in the door.

- **Identify course standards** including time required for outside work.

- **Use an icebreaker.** If possible, make it a question that is related to your course but without a specific answer.

- **Take care of housekeeping items** such as breaks and restroom locations.

- **Conduct a class with real course content.** It is important that students immediately understand that coming to class is a work situation with specific goals and purposes.

- Some successful instructors begin their first class by **asking students to write a short paragraph** about themselves and their concerns. Often students are willing to discuss their anxieties. This will help in understanding the class.

## Setting the Tone

Education professionals and teacher trainers agree that creating positive feelings about the course is an important goal for any instructor. Often instructors assume that students know they intend to be pleasant, cooperative, and helpful. However, this should not be taken for granted. With differing personalities and types of students in the classroom, faculty members must realize that a positive comment or gesture to one student may in fact be negative to another student. Thus, you should make a concerted effort to be friendly. A smile, a pleasant comment, or a laugh with students who are attempting to be funny will pay great dividends.

In setting the tone of the classroom, permissiveness is sometimes a good strategy. We are all familiar with the old classroom where students were essentially "passive" learners. We are also familiar with situations where excessive permissiveness became a distraction to other students. Teachers of adults must realize that flexibility and permissiveness are important to a proper learning environment and that encouraging creativity and unexpected comments is part of the learning and teaching process. The instructor has ultimate authority so excessive distraction can always be controlled. Instructors need not exercise authority for its own sake. Remember, permissiveness and flexibility requires considerable skill to work. Authority comes with the title of instructor.

## Teachers as Actors and Actresses

In reality, teachers are on stage; they are actors or actresses whether or not they recognize and admit it. A teacher in front of the classroom carries all of the responsibility for the success of the performance, and this requires all of the talents of anyone on the stage. Due to modern technology, unfortunately, students compare faculty to professionals they have seen in other roles. Thus, adjunct faculty must be alert to the ramifications of poor presentation. Faculty members have within themselves all of the emotions of stage performers but with greater audience interaction. There may occasionally be an emotional reaction in class and you should prepare for it. As an instructor, you will experience fear, joy, and feelings of tentativeness, but also feelings of extreme confidence and satisfaction. Handle fear with good preparation; confidence brought forward with good preparation is the easiest way to lessen fear. Remove anxieties from the classroom by developing communication systems. Some adjunct faculty members are effective at using humor.

 As a general rule, however, humor should be used delicately. Jokes are completely out. Almost any joke that is told will offend someone.

## Classroom Communication

Many kinds of communication exist in every classroom situation. You must be aware that facial expressions and eye contact with students as well as student interactions are all forms of communication. It is your responsibilty to ensure that classroom communication is structured in a positive manner. Communication starts the moment you enter the classroom for the first class session. The communication methods you use during the first class and the initial interaction with students are indicative of the types of communication that will exist throughout the course.

The amount of student participation as the course progresses is an indicator of the direction in which the communication is flowing; more is always better. Since many students today are adults, there is greater opportunity to call upon their experiences. The discussion of facts, events, examples, analogies, and anecdotes will often elicit an association for your adult students. This will encourage students to share experiences and anecdotes of their own.

Do not assume that classroom communication can only be between the instructor and students. Communication in the classroom can take any number of forms. It can mean a room full of small group activities where students are discussing and interacting with each other as the instructor stands silently by. It can also include animated and serious discussions and even disagreements while addressing a specific problem or issue presented in class. As the instructor, one of your major responsibilities is to provide a setting where students can communicate freely and provide an instructor-directed vehicle that maintains positive goal-oriented communication.

Some specific instructor-led communication activities include the use of open-ended questions, critical thinking techniques, anecdotes, and problem-solving activities. Communication activities between students include buzz groups, a partner system, student panels, collaborative learning activities, student group reports, brainstorming and group discussions. Remember, a good class is dynamic, participative, and interactive.

---

### The Three Rs of Teaching

Everyone remembers the three Rs of learning. For any instructor, however, the three Rs of teaching, are equally important.

The three Rs of good teaching are: **repeat, respond,** and **reinforce.** Very simply, student comments and contributions, if worthy of being recognized in class, are worthy of being repeated. A simple **repeat,** however, is not sufficient. You should elicit an additional **response** either from the class or the student making the original statement. After the response, you should offer a **reinforcement** of the statement or add your own conclusions. These three simple rules improve class relationships by emphasizing the importance of student contributions, relationships between students, and the instructor's respect for all the students. This promotes two-way communication and represents the application of one of the basic tenets of learning—**reinforcement.**

---

## Teaching Styles

Just as students have styles of learning, faculty have their own styles of teaching. Whether your style is one of planned preparation or a natural development, your style is important. For example, an instructor who emphasizes facts in teaching will have difficulty developing meaningful discussions with students who have progressed to the analysis stage of their learning. It is not important that part-time instructors modify their behavior to match that of students. It is important, however, that part-time faculty recognize their own teaching styles and adapt teaching processes, techniques, and strategies to enhance their most effective style. Some questions to assist you in determing your teaching style are:

- Do I tend to be authoritative, directional, semi-directional, or *laissez-faire* in my classroom leadership?

- Do I solicit communication with and between students easily or with difficulty?

- Am I well-organized and prepared?

- Am I meticulous in my professional appearance or do I have a tendency to put other priorities first and show up in class as is?

 A common mistake for many instructors is that they assume their students will learn in the same manner in which the instructor learned as a student.

Therefore, it would be wise to examine some of the basic learning styles of students, discussed in detail in Chapter 2. By understanding student learning styles, you can modify your teaching techniques to be certain that your presentation style does not turn off certain students.

For example, if you tended to learn best from a direct no-nonsense instructor, then chances are you will lean toward that type of behavior in your own teaching. This would satisfy students who learn in that manner; however, there will be students in your class who are more successful in a more *laissez-faire*-type environment that gives more freedom of expression. If you thrive on open communication and discussion in your learning process, expecting this from all of your students may be a false hope since many students are silent learners and may be intimidated by the need to verbally participate in class.

These are only a few examples of the types of teaching style adjustments that may be necessary to become an effective facilitator of learning. I have found that teaching styles are not static. Many of the techniques I used early in my career with younger students who appreciated humor and diversion were not as effective later with more mature students who felt they were there to learn, not to be entertained. I also noticed later in my career that although I was well-organized, had well-stated objectives, used good class communication, and observed the characteristics that I deemed important to good teaching, I had become too serious. For that reason I now occasionally mix in with my lesson plan an additional sheet that says to me, "smile, be friendly, smell the roses."

Also, I have found an evolution in the use of anecdotes. Strangely enough it was the reverse. Early in my career the use of anecdotes sometimes drew criticism from students as "too much story telling," or "more war stories." Later I began to put the question on my evaluation questionnaires: "Were the anecdotes and stories meaningful?" The overwhelming response from adult students was "yes." They were pertinent, they brought meaning to the class, and they were valuable because the adults were interested in real life experiences rather than rote lecturing.

*One note of caution, however, the use of anecdotes should relate to the topic being discussed and not simply stories of other experiences. In general, however, most of today's students will approve of anecdotes and may have their own to contribute.*

If you wish to do a quick analysis of your style, it can easily be done using the Internet. One such survey is "Gardner's Multiple Intelligences", available on most major search engines. This survey allows you to examine your strengths in eight categories, allowing you to analyze your own strengths and weaknesses in relation to your students. Although you need to be aware of copyright restrictions, many sites have surveys available with copyright permission granted so you can even use them in class.

A meaningful exercise might be to have your students complete the survey on their own (it is non-threatening) and discuss the composite results and what they mean in class.

## Professional Ethics

Although the teaching profession has been slow (compared to other professions) to address ethical issues, developments of the past few decades has encouraged an examination of the ethical status of college faculty. Although the recent attention has been inspired by legal or public relations concerns, there has always existed an unwritten code of ethics for teachers based upon values that have evolved both within the teaching profession and our culture.

> *Dr. Wilbert McKeachie states, "Ethical standards are intended to guide us in carrying out the responsibilities we have to the different groups with whom we interact"* (McKeachie, 1994).

Some institutions have adopted written standards of ethical behavior expected of all college faculty. A compilation of some of these standards is listed below as an example and all adjunct/part-time faculty should check with their department director or dean for information on their institution's standards. For clarity, the guidelines are presented in two categories: those pertaining to the profession of teaching and those pertaining to students.

*Ethics and the Profession.* This section is an attempt to emphasize the ethical expectations of the profession and the institution in which part-time faculty are employed.

Adjunct faculty:

- Will attend all assigned classes with adequately prepared materials and content as described in the course description.

- Will not attempt to teach a course for which they are not qualified and knowledgeable.

- Will present all sides on controversial issues.
- Will conduct a fair evaluation of students, applied equally to all.
- Will not promote outside entrepreneurial activities within the class setting.
- When reasonably possible, will attend college orientations and other development activities presented for the improvement of their role as an instructor.
- Will avoid behavior that may be interpreted as discriminatory based upon gender, age, social status or racial background.
- Will hold their colleagues and institution in highest respect in their actions and communication within and outside the institution.

*Professional Ethics and Students.* This section relates to ethical considerations concerning students.

Adjunct faculty:

- Will not discuss individual students and their problems outside of the professional structure of the institution.
- Will refer student personal problems to qualified staff.
- Will maintain and honor office hours and appointments with students.
- Will respect students' integrity and avoid social encounters with students which might suggest misuse of power.
- Will not attempt to influence students' philosophy or their positions concerning social and political issues.
- Will not ask students for personal information for research purposes.

These guidelines are quite general; however, they provide a vehicle for examining more closely the expectations of the institution in which you teach. Unfortunately, in today's world, there is sometimes a fine line between ethical issues and legal issues.

A more formal statement of professional standards is available from the National Education Association. For purposes of brevity, only the "Commitment to the Student" under the *Code of Ethics of the Education Profession* is presented here.

The educator strives to help each student realize his or her potential as a worthy and effective member of society. The educator therefore works to stimulate the spirit of inquiry, the acquisition of knowledge and understanding, and the thoughtful formulation of worthy goals.

In fulfillment of the obligation to the student, the educator—

- Shall not unreasonably restrain the student from independent action in the pursuit of learning.
- Shall not unreasonably deny the student's access to varying points of view.
- Shall not deliberately suppress or distort subject matter relevant to the student's progress.
- Shall make reasonable effort to protect the student from conditions harmful to learning or to health and safety.
- Shall not intentionally expose the student to embarrassment or disparagement.
- Shall not on the basis of race, color, creed, sex, national origin, marital status, political or religious beliefs, family, social or cultural background, or sexual orientation, unfairly:
  a. exclude any student from participation in any program.
  b. deny benefits to any student.
  c. grant any advantage to any student.
- Shall not use professional relationships with students for private advantage.
- Shall not disclose information about students obtained in the course of professional service unless disclosure serves a compelling professional purpose or is required by law (NEA, 1975).

## Academic Dishonesty

Academic dishonesty usually appears in two forms: either outright cheating or plagiarism. The problem of cheating in college classrooms has probably become more common in the last few years due to the pressures on students to succeed. Adding to the problem is the fact that we offer student instruction in conducting research on the World Wide Web, which in turn leads to temptation to copy materials from the Web rather than to conduct research.

To minimize cheating, some instructors place a significant percentage of the student evaluation in the form of shared or active student participation. These activities are evaluated for all members of the group, thus providing no incentive for individuals to attempt to cheat to better themselves. It is important also that in the classroom environment ethical responsibilities requiring trust and honesty are emphasized. Of course, the traditional method of countering cheating is to develop multiple tests with different questions and to not repeat the same test or test questions term after term.

Regardless of the amount of trust built in a classroom situation, all exams should be proctored and you should never leave the room in which an exam is being conducted. The instructor is ethically responsible for this commitment to the students who are striving honestly to achieve their goals and make their grade and to the institution. Obviously, extra time spent by the instructor to devise an evaluation plan in which written tests are only part of the final grade is time well spent. Lastly, on the final exam, students may be asked to write in their own words the two or three principles that affected them most in the course and what they feel they may gain in the future. This question could represent a significant part of the final grade.

If you suspect or encounter a student in the act of cheating or plagiarism, the student should be made aware of the situation. This should be done in confidence in a face-to-face meeting.

In the legalistic world we live in, there can only be one conclusive bit of advice: as an instructor, you must be aware of your institution's official procedures and the legal status of your position.

Suspecting someone of cheating or actually seeing is an unpleasant experience; however, it will likely happen in your teaching experience sooner or later. Usually, reasonable rational procedures will adequately cover the situation without the destruction of the student's academic career or standing.

## Checklist for Part-Time Faculty

There are many things that you need to know when receiving your teaching assignment. Each teaching situation may call for new information. There are, however, basic items that will almost assuredly be asked sometime during class. This section lists information you may wish to check before entering the first class.

(After reviewing this list, it is recommended that a personal timeline be developed including these and other important dates related to teaching the course.)

Figure 1.1—Faculty Checklist

## FACULTY CHECKLIST

1. What are the names of the department chairperson, dean, director and other important officials?

2. Have I completed all of my paperwork for official employment? (It's demoralizing when an expected paycheck doesn't arrive.)

3. Is there a pre-term faculty meeting?
   Date_____Time_____

4. Is there a departmental course syllabus, course outline, or statement of goals and objectives available for the course?

5. Are there prepared departmental handouts?

6. Are there prepared departmental tests?

7. Where is and/or how do I get my copy of the text(s) and support materials for teaching the class?

8. Is there a department and/or college attendance or tardiness policy?

9. When are grades due? When do students receive grades?

10. Is there a college or departmental grading policy?

11. Where can I get instructional aid materials and equipment, films, videotapes, software? What is the lead time for ordering?

12. Is there a student evaluation of instruction form for this course? Do I have or can I get a sample copy?

13. Where can I collect background and demographic information about students and their expectations?

14. Who are some of the other faculty who have taught the course? Are they open to assisting adjuncts?

15. Where can I find information to develop a list of resources and references pertaining to outside student assignments?

16. Have the course objectives been reviewed to be certain they reflect changes in text materials or technology?

17. Do I have a variety of instructional strategies planned so that my course does not become repetitious?

18. Do I have a current academic calendar that lists the length of term, the end of quarter, semester, or inter-term for special assignment so everyone clearly understands the beginning and termination of the course?

# CHAPTER 2
## TEACHING ADULT STUDENTS

Although it is impossible to prepare a standard plan that fits all classes, there are some fundamental principles and activities for teaching adult students. Keeping in mind that even these activities must be constantly reassessed to meet changing institutional and cultural needs, this chapter provides a better understanding of today's students so that an appropriate classroom assessment can be made.

### Student Characteristics

Today's students, whether they are older adults or just out of high school, possess some common expectations that effect classroom attitudes. These attitudes are based upon students viewing themselves as consumers of a product, rather than seekers of knowledge. As indicated earlier, they will expect well-planned and prepared course goals and objectives. Other recognizable characteristics include:

- Today's students are more self-directed than their earlier counterparts. In other words, they generally know what they want and where they are going.

- Today's students are highly demanding as consumers. They feel that, since they are paying for their education, they are entitled to a product. There have been legal cases in which colleges have been required to provide evidence of delivering advertised services (classes).

- Today's students often come to the classroom with rich life and educational experiences. They have read broadly and often have had interesting employment and/or travel experiences they may wish to share.

- Today's students expect to be treated as adults. They want to be treated as equals, not as students or "kids."

Although the students are more demanding, they are also more interesting, more challenging, and will contribute to a stimulating learning experience if given the opportunity. Most adult students are not in the classroom to compete. They are there to succeed and improve themselves. As a teacher of adults, you should minimize competition and increase cooperation to foster success. Above all, the age-old process of "x" number of A's, "x" number of B's, etc. based upon a bell curve, has been abandoned in the modern classroom.

### The Modern Student

The modern student is sometimes described as "the generation X student" or "X-gens." Many say that such a label is no more definitive than trying to describe a teenager. Those that dwell on the "generation X" concept often describe the students as bored and unmotivated, and having an "attitude" toward college that is resistant to disciplined study. These critics feel that the basis for this behavior is the students' desire for immediate gratification rather than establishing long-term goals.

A differing argument maintains that this kind of student has always been present in the classroom. There is, however, a significant intervening factor. The X-gen students have grown up surrounded by the influences of media, experiencing an inappropriately large amount of fantasy driven by television, movies, videos, and music. Add to this the advent of the Internet and one realizes that today's young students have come of age in a cultural environment vastly different from the typical student of the past. This environment has encouraged attitudes that may surface in the classroom in the form of consumer expectations and a lack of respect of authority. In addition, many of these students are the first generation known as "latchkey kids," children who grew up with both parents working. And to a far greater extent than in the past, many were raised in single-parent homes and/or are the product of divorce.

In order for you as a part-time instructor to challenge these students, it will be necessary to develop teaching strategies and procedures that will co-opt these learners. These active activities will include group work, role playing, cooperative learning and other techniques described later in Chapter 3. On the positive side, be aware that students today, although expecting a certain amount of autonomy, will respond to classroom activities in which they are involved and they see as meaningful. They will probably be interested in topics and work assignments that can be researched on the Internet rather than in print documents and periodicals from the library. To address their needs for immediate gratification, they will expect answers to their questions in class and comments and notes on their tests and quizzes.

 In planning your classroom strategies for the modern student, keep in mind that these students want *to do* something rather than *to know* something. Class presentation should incorporate a variety of format including charts, videos, graphics, computer projection and other technological visual aids.

## Teaching With the Techniques of Andragogy

If you are the typical part-time instructor today, you were probably first introduced to teaching using the methods of pedagogy. Pedagogy is based upon the teaching of children and is synonymous with the word "leader" (Knowles, 1990). In the past several years, however, the role of the teacher has changed from being a leader or presenter of learning to being a *facilitator* of learning because the average age of the college student today is closer to 30 than to the 20 years old of a few years ago. This older and more diverse student body will come to class motivated to learn but with a different set of needs. They are likely goal-oriented problem solvers and bring with them a need to know why they are learning something.

> Thus came the acceptance of the andragogical model pioneered by Knowles. The andragogical model is based upon:
> - *The student's need to know,*
> - *The learner's self concept,*
> - *The role of the learner's experience,*
> - *The readiness to learn,*
> - *An orientation to learning, and*
> - *Motivation.*

Andragogy has often been called the art and science of teaching adults because it places the student at the center of the learning process and emphasizes collaborative relationships among students and with the instructor—all techniques that work well with adult students. The andragogical model prescribes problem solving activities based upon the students' needs rather than on the goals of the discipline or the instructor.

Developing an andragogical teaching strategy requires a warm and friendly classroom environment to foster open communication. You must be aware that many adults have anxieties about their learning experience and lack confidence. Thus, plan activities that make students feel confident and secure with opportunities for students to share their experiences. It is important that this classroom environment be cultivated and nurtured in the first class session and that you establish yourself as a partner in learning and not an expert who has all the answers.

To incorporate the techniques of andragogy in your class, it is necessary that you become proficient in executing student-centered activities including: conducting a meaningful discussion, stimulating cooperative learning, developing good questions and critical thinking strategies, and involving all students in the learning process.

## Student-centered Learning

Student-centered learning is more than just implementation of adragogical strategies. As an adjunct faculty member, it would be wise for you to review your institution's mission statement or statement of philosophy. Many institutions in recent years have gravitated toward the concept of student- or client-centered learning. Institutionally, this may simply mean that the institution is striving to deliver their educational products to students anyplace at any time. Although the institution may be striving to meet the individual needs of the students, student-centered learning may or may not mean that the philosophy or purpose of the institution will change to adapt to all of the students' needs.

In the classroom, however, student-centered learning takes on a different meaning. Most contemporary institutions have adopted many educational delivery strategies to accommodate students in many ways in order to assist them in meeting their educational needs. In a learner-centered classroom, faculty are expected to implement strategies that allow students more self-determination in how they reach their goals. This objective is, however, tempered by the need of departments and disciplines to set explicit achievement standards that must be met to fulfill the goals of the academic discipline.

Some questions you may need to ask yourself to assess your goal of a student-centered learning environment are listed below.

- Do I have strategies to encourage **open communication** among students and between students and the teacher?
- Do I have appropriate **feedback mechanisms** in place so that the feelings and the needs of the students are communicated in a meaningful and timely manner?
- Do I have **collaborative learning strategies** in my lesson plans so students can work as teams, groups, or partners?
- Are the **needs of the students** being met along with the objectives of the course?
- Do I **recognize students as individuals** with diverse backgrounds and needs as well as classroom participants?

- Do I **vary my teaching strategie**s to accommodate a wide range of students?

Remember, a student-centered environment does not diminish the responsibility of the teacher nor give the students the power to determine course activities. Rather a student-centered environment requires skillful knowledge and use of cooperative and student-involved strategies implemented by the teacher.

## Student Learning Styles

One can easily find many paradigms for student learning styles in educational literature. Faculty are not expected to master or study in detail all of these styles and then attempt to categorize their students. It is, however, useful for you to understand some of the different learning styles that may appear in your classroom so that you can give consideration to individual differences. One such learning style system is called the "4mat system." This system identifies four types of learners. They are: imaginative learners, analytic learners, common sense learners, and dynamic learners.

- **Imaginative learners** will expect the faculty member to produce authentic curricula, to present knowledge upon which to build, to involve them in group work, and to provide useful feedback. They care about fellow students and the instructor.

- **Analytic learners** are more interested in theory and what the experts think, they need details and data, and are uncomfortable with subjectiveness. They expect the class to enhance their knowledge and place factual knowledge over creativity.

- **Common sense learners** test theories and look for practical applications; they are problem solvers and are typically skill oriented. They expect to be taught skills and may not be flexible or good in teamwork situations.

- **Dynamic learners** believe in self-discovery. They like change and flexibility, are risk takers, and are at ease with people. They may, however, be pushy and manipulative. They respond to dynamic instructors who are constantly trying new things (McCarthy, 1987).

It is important to understand that all or some of these types of learners may be present in any given class. This makes it necessary for the instructor to possess the ability to use a variety of classroom activities.

I recall an experience while teaching that relates to this topic. Having for years been successful in teaching classes by encouraging open communication and maximizing student involvement, I found myself teaching a class in which an acquaintance was enrolled. This person simply would not respond or take part in discussions. Knowing the student to be social and bright, I was not completely surprised that when all the criteria for grades were considered, the individual easily earned an "A," contrary to my belief that all students must participate to learn! It was only later that I realized that the student process for learning was not flawed, it was just different from the style that I, as the instructor, had perceived necessary for learning.

Closely reviewing the description of the student types will bring out another important factor. That is, just as students have learning styles, teachers have teaching styles. Thus, you should be able to identify your own teaching style from the learning style descriptions. Understanding your teaching style will allow you to modify your behavior to accommodate all learners.

After considering the learning styles above, it is just as important to keep in mind two major factors concerning adult learners. First, they have basically been trained to be cognitive learners so they will first seek to obtain the knowledge and information that they feel is necessary to complete the course work and receive a passing grade. Second, adults learn by doing. They want to take part in learning activities based upon their needs and application. When interacting with individual students in your classroom, you must continually recognize that all learners are not coming from the same set of circumstances.

## Diversity in the Classroom

If there is any area of teaching that demands common sense, it is the diversity found in today's classrooms. Classes today are full of students of various age groups, ethnic backgrounds, cultural experiences, and educational abilities. This diversity can contribute to a more interesting classroom when interactive learning allows students to learn about different cultures and differing perspectives first hand through debate and discussion.

For the teacher, however, diversity poses significant challenges. While you must be aware of your students' diverse backgrounds, you must be equally cautious not to overcompensate or appear to give special attention to any one group or individual.

There are some specific teaching strategies that can be implemented and of which you should be aware. When contemplating the course content you should consider the age of the students and their experiences. For example, when older students contribute anecdotes, they usually use their own past experiences. While younger students may prefer topics that effect them immediately. In understanding student attitudes and behaviors, keep in mind that many older students were educated in structured classroom settings and are accustomed to formal lecture and discussion formats, while younger students will probably respond to a more active learning style. Older students also will have the confidence to share their experiences and backgrounds with the class whereas younger students may hesitate.

Above all avoid stereotyping any members of our culture. Solomon (1994) makes specific suggestions concerning diversity in the classroom. Some of his suggestions are:

- Do not address students by a preferred name. Learn to pronounce their correct name.
- Do not tell or tolerate racist, sexist, ethnic or age-related jokes.
- Do not imply negatives when addressing other ethnic groups or culturally different societies.
- Become aware of your own prejudices.

- Never allow your own personal values to be the sole basis for judgment.

- Constantly evaluate your cultural perceptions to be sure they are not based upon personal insecurities.

Generally keep in mind that the diverse classroom provides several opportunities. Diversity provides an enriching experience when students share with each other and with the instructor and may assist in reducing cultural barriers. The diverse class provides a forum for understanding the differences that exist between individuals and social classes. Through group interactive strategies, these differences can give students the chance to be full participants in their learning and development process. These group strategies can also provide opportunities for all students to become a part of their classroom community regardless of their background.

## Bloom's Taxonomy of Educational Objectives

If there is a single paradigm that has stood the test of time in education it is Benjamin Bloom's *Taxonomy of Educational Objectives* (Bloom et al., 1956). Published nearly a half a century ago, this taxonomy describes the learning process as three factors or domains. They are the cognitive domain, affective domain, and psychomotor domain.

Essentially, cognitive learning is learning that emphasizes knowledge and information and incorporates analysis of that knowledge. Affective learning centers on values and value systems, receiving stimuli, ideas and to some degree, organization. Psychomotor learning addresses hand/eye coordination, normally referred to as physical coordination.

The importance of these three domains is not so much the overall consideration of the categories as it is the breakdown provided by Bloom. For example, Bloom's cognitive domain is broken into several categories: knowledge, comprehension, application, analysis, synthesis, and evaluation. The affective domain is broken into receiving, responding, valuing, organizing and characterization of value complex. A psychomotor domain essentially is that which provides for the development of physical skills.

The cognitive domain is usually emphasized in the classroom learning situation. However, when writing course objectives it is often expected that all three domains will be represented. This means that you should have objectives in the cognitive domain written not only at the knowledge level but also the evaluation, analysis, and synthesis levels. In the affective domain, you would have objectives covering responding, valuing and value complex. Many institutions require course objectives and activities in all three of the domains of Bloom's Taxonomy. It should be noted from examination of the descriptions rendered here that these domains effectively cover all areas of the learning process.

## Motivation

Students are motivated for many reasons: individual improvement, intellectual curiosity, needed employment competencies, career change or advancement, employment requirement, or the completion of degree or certificate requirements. Although these motivational reasons are broad and varied, faculty must possess the skills to motivate students with a variety of activities including occasional risk-taking.

The following anecdote exemplifies such risk taking. After many years of teaching, I remember being faced with a class that would not respond or participate. Admittedly it was a Friday night class; however, you might expect that in such a class, highly motivated students would be enrolled. They were, however, very tired students and many of them were enrolled merely to pick up additional credits. After teaching the class about three weeks and experiencing very little student response, on the spur of the moment during the third evening, I simply stated, "We must start communicating. I would like each of you at this time to turn to a person near you, introduce yourself and tell them that you are going to help them get through the course, no matter how difficult it is, that you will be there to help them whenever they become confused, and that the two of you (by helping each other) can be successful in this course." This seemingly simple technique worked wonders. The students became acquainted with someone they hadn't previously known, and in many cases, found someone who really could help them get through the course. For the remainder of the course, when it appeared that the class was experiencing difficulty, I simply needed to say "let's take a few minutes and get together with our partner." When chalkboard work was given, two students would voluntarily go to the board together. Thus a previously unused "risk" activity proved successful—and was my first experience with collaborative learning and the partner system. This is an example of trying a basic technique of motivation. In this case it worked. It may not work every time, but it was not a technique that I had in my repertoire prior to that time. So, when motivating adult students, remember that you must occasionally try techniques not necessarily found in the literature; however, there are proven techniques that should be in the professional portfolio of all teachers, such as Maslow's Hierarchy of Needs.

## Maslow's Hierarchy of Needs

It is virtually impossible to incorporate all theories of motivation for your students. It is appropriate, therefore, that we find refuge in a time-honored theory of learning called Maslow's Hierarchy of Needs. Maslow's hierarchy states that the basic needs of human beings fall into five categories:

- *PHYSIOLOGICAL—feeling good physically with appropriate food and shelter.*
- *SAFETY—the feeling of security in one's environment.*
- *LOVE AND BELONGING OR THE SOCIAL NEED—fulfilling the basic family and social role.*
- *ESTEEM—the status and respect of a positive self-image.*
- *SELF-ACTUALIZATION—growth of the individual.*

*Physiological, Safety, Love and Belonging.* The fact that Maslow's needs are in hierarchy form is a major problem for teachers of adults. For example, attempting to address the needs of esteem and self-actualization in the classroom, when physiological, safety, and love and belonging needs have not been met, is a difficult task. In fact, the lack of fulfillment of the basic needs may interfere with the learning process. This interference may manifest itself in anti-social behavior.

The challenge becomes, how does one in a short period of time, teaching on a part-time basis to mostly part-time students, overcome these barriers? The fact is that one may not overcome all of these barriers. If instructors attempt to take the time to analyze each of the unmet needs of each of their students, they will have little time to work toward the goals and objectives of the course.

 There is, however, an important factor to support the instructor. It is that the need to achieve appears to be a basic need in human beings. The need to succeed, an intrinsic motivator that usually overcomes most of the other distractions to learning, is the factor upon which successful teachers capitalize.

There is little that faculty can do to help students to meet the physiological, safety, and love and belonging needs. The need for esteem and self-actualization, which are essentially achievement, are areas in which teaching strategies can be implemented.

*Esteem.* Esteem is the status and respect with which human beings are regarded by their peers and activities faculty members incorporate that assist students in achieving status and self-respect will support fulfillment of the esteem need. This is accomplished by providing an environment in which students can experience success in their learning endeavors. *Many learning theorists claim that success in itself is the solution to motivation and learning.*

One of the great fallacies of teaching is often stated by students who have succeeded in classes where other students have dropped out. That observation is: "That prof. was tough, but he/she was really good." This may or may not be true. *The fact is that being tough has absolutely no relationship to being good.* Too often the reverse of this statement is perpetuated when some faculty emphasize toughness as a substitute for good teaching. There is no evidence to suggest that "tough teachers" are better teachers than those who are "not so tough." It is especially discouraging to marginal students who are working hard but find the chances for success negated by the instructor's desire to be tough.

Building esteem through success is accomplished in many ways. The following are some classroom instruction suggestions to assist students in achieving success:

- *Make certain that students are aware of course requirements.* Students should be provided with course objectives in written form that tell them what they are expected to accomplish.

- *Inform students precisely what is expected of them.* This means not only the work or the skills necessary for them to complete the course content, but also the time commitment.

- *Give students nonverbal encouragement whenever possible.* There are many ways this can be accomplished. Eye contact with students can very often elicit a positive response. Gestures are important. A smile, a nod of the head, just looking at students with the feeling that you find the classroom a pleasant environment is in itself effective nonverbal encouragement.

- *Give positive reinforcement at every opportunity.* Simple techniques such as quizzes for which grades are not taken, quizzes designed so most or all students will succeed, as well as short tests as a supplement to grading are effective positive reinforcement strategies. Comments written on hand-in papers, tests, and projects are effective ways to provide positive feedback. Of course, the ideal form of positive reinforcement is provided through individual conferences and informal conversations with students at chance meetings.

- *Provide a structured situation in which the students feel comfortable.* The *laissez-faire* classroom is generally a lazy classroom. Most educators agree that a structured setting with students participating in activities is much better than an unstructured approach.

- *Provide opportunity for student discussion of outside experiences.* Some students in your class, who may not be particularly adept in the course content, may have significant contributions and accomplishments to share. One of the greatest builders of esteem is to allow students to share their success experiences with others.

*Self-Actualization.* Self-actualization, the highest of Maslow's hierarchy, is the realization of individual growth. Such growth is realized through achievement and success. Course planning for enhancement of student self-actualization is the ultimate in successful teaching. The suggestions listed here can assist in the student growth process.

- *Each class should offer a challenge to each student.* Challenges are presented in a variety of ways. If they are insurmountable challenges they become barriers; therefore, it is important that faculty plan activities appropriate for the course. Grades are challenges. However, grades must be achievable or they cause frustration. Achieving class credit is a challenge. Most students, even though they may not achieve the grade desired, will feel satisfied if they obtain the credit for which they are working. Assigning incompletes and allowing additional time for projects are techniques that will assist students in obtaining credit for their work. Questions, if properly phrased, can become challenges.

- *Problem solving.* The ultimate challenge in the classroom is problem solving. Problem-solving techniques vary greatly depending upon the subject matter. Although it is impossible to discuss in detail the ramifications of problem solving, this challenge does not lend itself solely to scientific and mathematics classes. It can also be utilized in many other courses through discussion, professional journals and literature reports, outside projects, case studies, and group work.

- *Treat students as individuals.* Individual conferences and development of a system to promote interaction between students, their instructor, and other students are important. Many experienced faculty members do not hesitate to share with students their home or business phone number and/or e-mail address and are usually quite surprised at how seldom any are used.

- *Be cautious not to prejudge students.* Unfortunately, stereotyping still exists today. Faculty must make every effort not to "type" classes or students as "good" or "bad." Such stereotyping will affect grading and attitudes toward the students. Also, there is a good chance that the judgment may be incorrect. *There is no place for stereotypes in education.*

- *Treat students as adults.* Many of today's students hold powerful positions in business and industry. It is difficult for them to regard the teacher as someone superior. To adult students, the instructor is just someone in a different role. Above all, don't refer to them as "kids."

- *Give consideration to student's personal problems when possible.* Giving adult students personal consideration implies that rules concerning attendance, paper deadlines, tardiness, etc., may be flexible when faced with the realities of the lives of adult students. Practice flexibility whenever possible.

# CHAPTER 3
## CLASSROOM STRATEGIES
## FOR TEACHING ADULTS

### Teacher Behaviors

Adjunct faculty can assist student learning with tried and proven strategies. Some principles and strategies to remember are:

- *The teacher is a facilitator of learning.* Students do not expect teachers to know all there is to know about the subject. They do expect, however, the teacher to facilitate learning the facts and skills of the course.

- *Understand your teaching situation.* As an adjunct faculty member you may have a variety of assignments at different institutions. When making your class preparations, consider the following questions: Is this class part of a competitive program? Are the goals clarified for the student and the institution? Can student projects be developed to meet the students' needs?

- *Allow for individual differences.* Every classroom will contain a diverse group of individuals. Allow for this by giving individual help, knowing students' names, and being aware of differing backgrounds.

- *Vary teaching activities.* Use different activities in the classroom. Try new ideas. Some experts recommend changing activities every 20 minutes.

- *Develop a supportive climate.* Students should understand that you are there to support them in the learning process not to prove how tough the course is.

- *Be sensitive to barriers.* Some of the baggage students bring with them include: unsuccessful previous educational experience, time restraints, confusion concerning college (procedures) in general, failure to understand their academic limitations, stress, physical and mental handicaps.

- *Be a learning partner.* Communicate to the students that you are a partner in their learning. You will develop and work with them on strategy, materials, and projects that will allow them to self direct their learning experience.
- *Emphasize experimentation.* Emphasize to the students that trying new learning techniques and making mistakes are often as valuable as reaching the right conclusion immediately.
- *Use technology to enhance learning.* Know about and be able to use the latest learning technologies such as computers and the Internet.

Most of all it is important that you be understanding and considerate. With dynamic changes in the educational field today, you need to keep up with these technological and cultural changes so that they become part of the teaching/learning process. Being alert to these changes will prevent the worst student criticism, "it isn't done that way anymore."

## Student Behaviors

During your teaching tenure you will experience differing classroom behavior from students that may challenge your ability to maintain the class in a constructive and positive manner. Keep in mind that the following suggestions are simply observations of other teachers and may not apply to all situations.

- *The class expert.* This person has all or most of the answers and is more than willing to share them—and will argue if he or she is not right. Suggestion: Make eye contact with a different student in the class and ask for an opinion. Allow other students to react. Give respondent time to tell anecdotes and/or present position, then remind the "expert" and the class that they must get back to the objectives of the course.

- *The quiet class.* Give positive reinforcement to any response from any student. Change teaching strategies and request an answer to a simple question at the beginning of the next class session. Use questioning techniques, group work, partner system, current events, personal experiences, brainstorming, or icebreakers.

- *The talkative class.* Direct a question to a group or supportive individual. Quiet class to recognize an individual to make their point or position known. Validate or invalidate point and move to the next topic in the lesson plan. Allow time for conversation, specify time for class work to begin, exert your control.

- *The negative student.* Initially ignore! Invite the student to a conference, provide success experience, determine an interest of student and cultivate it.

- *The off-the-subject student.* Allow some freedom for discussion and for the reaction of other students. Other students will usually provide incentive to get back on subject. Seize the opportunity and stress the need to get back to course objectives.

- *The unruly student.* Remain calm and polite. Above all keep your cool and your temper. Don't disagree. Try to determine the student's position and his or her reason for concern. Listen intently and allow the student an opportunity to verbally withdraw from the situation.

 If angry, try to determine the basis of the anger the student is expressing. Ask the individual to meet with you privately during the break and if necessary call an immediate break. As a last resort the class may be dismissed and institutional procedures for such a situation should be implemented. *Keep in mind that your primary responsibility is the safety of all students.* If procedures are not established, inquire of your institution why they are not.

## Classroom Assessment

One of the most recent and dynamic classroom strategies is termed "classroom assessment." Basically, classroom assessment is an ongoing sophisticated feedback mechanism that carries with it specific implications in terms of learning and teaching. It can be used in large or small classes, in any type of class and at any level. Classroom assessment techniques can be used daily or periodically, at the beginning of the course or at the end. The techniques emphasize the principles of active learning as well as student-centered learning.

Specifically, classroom assessment techniques answer the questions: "what are students learning and how effectively am I teaching?"

Classroom assessment techniques are truly developmental, in that no credit should ever be granted for assessment activities. Using classroom assessment is closer to doing classroom research than to developing pedagogical or andragogical techniques. They are intended to provide teachers with a continuous flow of information on student learning and the quality of instruction in the classroom.

The recognized founders of classroom assessment movement, T.A. Angelo and K.P. Cross, discuss in significant detail assessment practices that can be implemented by the teacher. In *Classroom Assessments, A Handbook for College Teachers, second edition* (Angelo and Cross, 1993), they provide a detailed analysis of assessment as well as its philosophical and procedural background. For this brief description of classroom assessment, three of the most popular and common techniques presented by Angelo and Cross are outlined. They are called: the minute paper, the muddiest point, and the one-sentence summary.

*The minute paper*, sometimes known as the one-minute paper or the minute response, is a quick and effective way to collect written feedback from the students. It is simple to use, opens communication with students, and provides an active learning activity. To use the minute paper, the instructor merely stops the class two or three minutes early and asks the students to respond to two questions: (1) what is the most important thing you learned in today's class? and (2) what is the most important thing that remain unanswered or leave questions in your mind? Students write their responses on small sheets of paper or on cards and turn them in to the instructor as they leave the class.

The minute paper question, of course, can be worded in several different ways. If one is asking about the understanding of a problem-solving activity, it can be specified. The minute paper is then used at the introduction of the following class for either opening a discussion of the most noted minute paper responses or presenting the questions and answers that are most relevant. There is no need to ask students to identify themselves on the minute paper since the intent is to assess understanding.

*The muddiest point.* The muddiest point, unlike the minute paper, asks students to respond to a single question. The muddiest point asks the students to identify what they are *not* getting from the class or are *not understanding.* The instructor can specify whether they wish the student to respond to the lecture, a demonstration, or general problem-solving activity. Leaving the muddiest point unsigned and having them dropped in a box as the students leave the class relieves the student of any concerns they might have about their relationship with the instructor and provides an efficient avenue of input to the instructor.

*The one-sentence summary.* The one-sentence summary requires the students to provide additional information, actually reaching the synthesis level of Bloom's Taxonomy. The one-sentence summary asks students to answer the question "who does what to whom, when, where, how, and why" about the topic and then to analyze those answers in a simple long summary sentence. This technique should be used with important topics and principles, and works well in chronologically organized classes where students need to have some command of elementary principles and processes before moving onto a more advanced topic.

Use of classroom assessment techniques requires the instructor to first determine the goals and objectives of the course, the basic principles the students must learn to succeed in the course, and what types of examples students are required to complete or analyze.

## Critical Thinking

Critical thinking can best be stimulated by raising questions and by offering challenges about a specific issue or statement. Many students still like the "right" answer from the instructor but critical thinking in instruction goes far beyond that. Critical thinking involves asking the right kinds of questions and goes so far as to let students develop assumptions and analyze (either in groups or individually) those assumptions. They can then examine alternatives to their assumptions.

Some types of questions to ask might be: "What is the source of your information and how reliable is it?" "What are your personal experiences in relation to the information?" "What are the different positions?" "What are your feelings on the topic?" "Why?" "Do you agree?" Allow students time to think and wait for some response. If students take a position on an issue, ask them for an alternate position.

## Feedback

As has been indicated in other parts of this publication, obtaining student feedback is instrumental to good instruction. Most instructors rely upon student questions and responses in class for their feedback. Good feedback, however, is too important to leave to chance.

The faculty evaluation form that follows and the section on "Quality Circles" in this publication are examples of feedback. The institution in which you teach may have prepared instruments that can be of value. All such documents have weaknesses as well as strengths, whether they be open-ended or close-ended questions, rating forms or checklists. Given the time constraints facing most adjunct faculty, there are a few techniques that provide immediate and helpful feedback. They are:

- Prior to testing, give the class sample test questions which are not counted toward the grade, and ask them to write responses to the questions as well as the content.

- Maintain open and ongoing verbal communication, especially concerning clarity of assignments and deadlines.

- At the end of the course, have the students write a letter to "Aunt Millie" describing the course to her, then collect it.

- Do not confuse feedback with evaluation. Feedback is an opportunity for you to relate to your students and to enhance your class.

---

Some additional methods for obtaining feedback are:

| | |
|---|---|
| *class discussion* | *study guides* |
| *group discussions* | *course post-mortem* |
| *student conferences* | *paper comments* |
| *quizzes* | *quality circles* |

---

## Faculty Self-Evaluation

Many colleges today have forms available for faculty who wish to conduct self-evaluations in addition to the official course evaluations for the institution or academic department. Whether voluntary or mandatory, keep in mind that most of these evaluation forms in fact capture student opinion and are not statistically valid. This does not, however, decrease the value of seeking student input to improve teaching. Whether you are an experienced faculty member or new to the profession, you will invariably find surprises while conducting such evaluations.

New faculty members will be astonished at the quality of some observations students make. I recall an acquaintance whose associates thought he had an effective sense of humor. However, after conducting a classroom evaluation, he was surprised to find that the students not only rated him low, but many felt he did not possess a sense of humor.

 Whether or not the results of student samplings of this type precipitate a change in faculty behavior is not always important. It is important, however, that faculty know how they are being perceived by the students.

There are two identifiable characteristics that are consistently valued by the students in relation to faculty behavior: a) demonstrating business-like behavior in the classroom, and b) being understanding and friendly.

Below is a form that you may use to conduct self-evaluation. Note that the form exists in two sections: classroom factors and personal factors.

The first section of the form (classroom evaluation) collects student insights into classroom behavior. The final section (personal factors) gives you an opportunity to select personal characteristics that you may wish to review and on which students may want to comment. Questions may be added or deleted to this form at will.

Remember that student perceptions are very often motivated by personal biases, rather than objective evaluation of the instructor; however, continued use of such a form helps to determine if there are characteristics that continue to surface that need attention. Many statistical techniques can be applied to evaluation forms such as this. A simple method of utilizing this form is to ask the students to assign numbers 1-5 to each of the categories and then weigh them on a number scale. It is not intended that this self-evaluation form have content validity; however, it will give faculty members insight into their teaching.

Figure 3.1—Faculty Evaluation Form

# Faculty Evaluation Form

Class_____     Date_____

*Instructions: Grade each factor on a scale of 1-5 your perception of the teacher's behavior or characteristics. (low=1; high=5, NA for not applicable).*

### Classroom Factors

| | |
|---|---|
| Preparation for class | _____ |
| Communication of expectations to students | _____ |
| Command of subject matter | _____ |
| Course objectives clearly defined | _____ |
| Course content clearly reflects catalog description | _____ |
| Instructor encouraged student involvement | _____ |
| Instructor was professional and business-like | _____ |
| Instructor well prepared and organized | _____ |
| Tests reflected classroom presentation and objectives | _____ |
| Instructor utilized student-centered techniques | _____ |
| Instructor willing to give individual help | _____ |
| Instructor utilized technology and instructional aids | _____ |

### Instructor's Personal Factors

| | |
|---|---|
| Considerate of differing opinions | _____ |
| Considerate of students with differing backgrounds | _____ |
| Personal appearance | _____ |
| Friendly and helpful to individual students | _____ |
| Overall rating | _____ |

Greatest strengths_____

_____

Greatest weaknesses_____

_____

Suggestions to improve course_____

_____

(This form may be reproduced in its entirety if desired.)

# CHAPTER 4
## PLANNING FOR INSTRUCTION

Of all the duties of part-time faculty, from lecturing to grading tests, the single most important is planning. Good planning is *essential* to successful teaching. Many of your students will come from structured backgrounds or employment situations where plans and performance objectives are expected. In addition, over the past several years, legal action has been taken against institutions that promised a high quality education in their product advertisement, accusing them of failure to provide this "product" to their student "customers." The best defense against this kind of action is a viable written plan.

Good planning requires a comprehensive approach, beginning with the course description and ending with the students' evaluation. Executing the plan for a course is much like a football game. Nearly everyone knows the standard plays and the standard procedures; the execution is what determines success.

Planning must take place prior to the first class. The preliminary steps include: becoming familiar with the text, organizing the material into content areas and topics, and prioritizing goals and objectives. Each of the major topics must be assigned class time and a plan designed for the activities associated with each topic. In addition, instructors should develop "fillers" for class sessions when additional material is needed.

---

Good planning includes several documents. They include:

- *Written Course Objectives*
- *A Course Outline*
- *A Course Syllabus*
- *Lesson Plans*

---

## Writing Course Objectives

Appropriate objectives for every college course based on the course description and institution-given goals, are not an option for any faculty. No longer is there dialogue about whether or not college courses will have objectives; all courses and classes must have them. Faculty success depends largely upon their ability to develop and implement course objectives. The flowchart below indicates the major components of the teaching/planning process.

The most important activity in this process is developing appropriate course objectives.

Fortunately, the development of good course objectives is not as complex and difficult as one might expect.

There do exist, however, two remaining pitfalls:

• The tendency to write more objectives than can be covered in class, and

• The tendency to write objectives that are not clear to the student.

There are two very simple techniques to overcome these problems. First, in order to avoid writing objectives in a haphazard manner, simply develop the course goals and write the objectives for the goals rather than for the course. The course goals will be based on the course description the institution places in its catalog. Once you have written the goals, write objectives to support each goal. Don't worry about the ramifications of low priority objectives. A simple format is to write one goal at the top of a separate sheet of paper and then detail that goal's objectives underneath.

Avoiding the second pitfall, clarity of understanding, begins with using clearly understood descriptors when writing the objectives. Objectives should be few but concise. Begin developing appropriate objectives by verbalizing and writing your thoughts concerning the objective.

After writing down the objective statement, rewrite it and apply these appropriate descriptors:

| | |
|---|---|
| write | solve |
| contrast | compare |
| compose | describe |
| compute | identify |
| list | attend |

When writing objectives, remember that you must be able to measure whether or not the objective has been reached.

Conversely, descriptors that should not be used since they cannot be clearly measured include:

| | |
|---|---|
| understand | appreciate |
| enjoy | believe |
| grasp | discuss |

Conditional lead-ins, such as "at the completion of…" aren't necessary since these are understood. Some conditions may be included, for example, the achievement of a certain rating score or the completion of a certain activity in a given time. Make every effort, however, to be clear so students understand all conditions. Good objectives are essential to a good planning process.

> *You should evaluate and assign grades based on the completion of the course objectives.*

Robert Mager, one of the pioneers of the instructional objective movement, outlines several principles to be observed in writing objectives:

- *be explicit,*
- *communicate,*
- *tell what the learner will be doing,*
- *indicate conditions if there are any,*
- *include some recognition of successful completion* (Mager, 1962).

Examples of some well-written objectives are:

- The student *will recite* the Gettysburg Address.

- The student *will identify* the major components of a successful lesson plan.

- The student *will describe* the process involved in a bank approval of a consumer loan.

- The student *will write* a five-page news release on a selected topic with a minimum of two errors.

Some institutions may require the development of objectives based upon Bloom's *Taxonomy of Educational Objectives*. This taxonomy provides that instruction be organized around one or more of the hierarchy of objectives. They are: knowledge, comprehension, application, analysis, synthesis and evaluation (Bloom *et al.*, 1956). If objectives are prepared across this hierarchy, you need to recognize that your objectives and the teaching strategies to achieve them can not be limited to the knowledge level where only information recall is required. You must develop instructional plans and activities that ensure students achieve competencies in the application, analysis, and synthesis domains. More active teaching styles will incorporate the higher order objectives that ensure students are able to reach the objectives described.

## The Course Outline

While the course objectives give you the conceptual overview of the upcoming class, the course outline is much more comprehensive and allows you to flesh out the entire course by applying detail to the objectives.

The course outline usually uses the standard outline format to cover the topics from the course objectives. Generally, a topic should not be divided into more than three subtopics for a course outline. If there are more than three subtopics, place them in the daily lesson plan.

---

*The purpose of the outline is very simple: to make certain that all major topics are recognized and addressed during the course.*

---

The two types of outlines most commonly used in teaching are the chronological outline and the content outline. The chronological outline is used for courses that lend themselves to time or historic sequence. Sequential courses; such as mathematics, history, and science where previous knowledge is necessary to function at a higher level; require chronological outlines.

Content outlines are used with topics taught in a specified content order and is often called a topical outline. This allows considerable flexibility since you may arrange the course in the way that you consider most effective for presentation. For example, physical education faculty may allow students to actually perform an activity prior to its being taught so that the students can see a need for the techniques. Whereas, a chronological outline calls for the presentation of the basic information before students attempt to perform the operation. A course concerned with legislative, judicial, or community activities may not require that field trips to legislative bodies or courtrooms be conducted in sequence with other activities in the course.

Although in most institutions, there are course outlines available, generally they will not be maintained as formal documents.

Often, outlines are treated in the same manner as lesson plans—that is—something the instructor develops. (The formal document recognized at most institutions and approved by the college is the course syllabus). A sample course outline is shown in figure 4.1. Theoretically, a proper course outline is developed in conjunction with the course objectives. This assures direction and purpose of the outline.

## Figure 4.1—Sample Course Outline

**Achievement University**
**Basic Statistics 101 Course Outline**

I. **Introduction**
   A. Basic statistics—use and purposes
   B. Data gathering
      1. Instruments
      2. Recorded data
      3. Machine utilization
II. **Presenting Data**
   A. Tables
      1. Summary tables
         a. Table elements
         b. Tables with averages
   B. Graphs
      1. Types of graphs
         a. Bar
         b. Pie chart
         c. Line graph
      2. Data presentation with graphs
   C. Frequency distributions
      1. Discrete and continuous
      2. Class intervals
III. **Descriptions and Comparison of Distributions**
   A. Percentiles
      1. Computation of percentile
      2. Inter-percentile range
      3. Percentile score
   B. Mean and standard deviations

1. Computation of mean
       a. From grouped data
       b. From arbitrary origin
   2. Variance formulas

C. Frequency distributions
       1. Measures of central tendency
       2. Symmetry and skews
       3. Bimodal distributions

**IV. Predictive or Estimate Techniques**
   A. Regression
       1. Graphic application
       2. Assumption of linearity
   B. Correlation
       1. Computation of correlation coefficient
       2. Reliability of measurement
   C. Circumstances affecting regression and analysis
       1. Errors of measurement
       2. Effect of range
       3. Interpretation of size

**V. The Normal Curve and Statistical Inference**
   A. The normal distribution
       1. Mean
       2. Standard deviation
       3. Characteristics
   B. Statistical inference
       1. Employing samples
           a. Randomness
           b. Parameters
       2. Normal Distribution
           a. Standard errors
           b. Unbiased estimate
           c. Confidence interval
   C. Testing hypothesis
       1. Definition of statistical hypothesis
       2. Test of hypothesis
           a. Level of significance
           b. One-sided test
       3. Computing power of test

## The Course Syllabus

A syllabus is defined in the dictionary as "*a concise statement of the main points of a course of study or subject.*" Although this definition leaves room for interpretation, i.e. what constitutes "concise" and what constitutes "the main points," one thing is certain: *the syllabus is the official document of the course.*

---

*As a permanent contribution to the institution's instructional archives, your syllabus is a contract between the institution and your students with the completion of the syllabus requirements determining their course grade. Thus, it is probably the most important document in the educational process.*

---

Confusion in academia concerning syllabi arises when faculty members interpret the word syllabus differently. For example, a concise statement to one faculty member may simply mean "Chapter V." Whereas to another faculty member the concise statement may mean enumerating the major points of Chapter V, describing each point, and writing a complete sentence for each. Often, you will have access to other syllabi for the course you are teaching on which you can base your own course syllabus.

However, sometimes part-time faculty will encounter situations where a syllabus is not available. There are two reasons for this: course development and presentation have been left completely to an individual faculty member who is not required to provide this information to the institution, or part-time faculty may be teaching a new or recently revised course for which no syllabus has been developed. In either case, with or without sample syllabi, you must construct a syllabus for your course.

Development of the syllabus is a multi-step process. A good syllabus has several major parts:

- The complete name of the course, including the course number and catalog description

- The name and title by which the faculty member wishes to be addressed

- The faculty member's office hours

- The text(s) and other materials required

- The course objectives

- The student assignments and projects

- The course requirements and grading standards

- A complete listing of resources, outside readings, and field trips

- The evaluation plan

Items one through four are self-explanatory or should be available from the academic department staff. However, items five through nine require some explanation.

- **Course Objectives.** The first major part of the syllabus is the presentation of the course objectives. Listing the objectives for a course is often difficult for new faculty members. The tendency is to include everything you think is important to the course. This dilutes the objectives and often makes them too confusing or overwhelming for the student. As a rule, most courses can be adequately described by developing not more than ten to fourteen objectives.

> *One must be certain, however, that the objectives are reachable, teachable, and that student learning activities can be directed to each.*

- **Student Activities.** Following the course objectives, the syllabus should describe the student activities needed to meet the course requirements, including detailed specific activities, such as outside reading, laboratory activities, projects, and other assignments. Describe these activities in a way that relates directly to the objectives. Significant attention should be given to the reasons for the activities and how they relate to the course. This approach tells students that the class is all business and that there is a purpose for everything.

- **Course Requirements.** Next, the syllabus should include a detailed description of the course requirements and student responsibilities. This is one of the most important parts of the syllabus because it defines exactly what is expected to succeed in the class. It eliminates the possibility that students will claim ignorance of what was expected. In fact, it is useful in this section of the syllabus to list the class meetings by day and date as well as the reading and homework assignments and class topics to be addressed each meeting. Many experienced faculty members have felt that this detail was not necessary until they found themselves in an indefensible position concerning student accusations that the course content was not adequately covered. Sometimes this section of the syllabus is broken into two or more parts; the general rule is that excessive detail is better than too little detail.

- **Resources and References.** Finally, the syllabus should include a complete list of resources, outside readings, bibliographies, and other outside activities. Required outside readings and library reserve assignments should be specified. You need not be concerned if the syllabus eventually grows into a document of several pages. The students will appreciate your efforts, and you will be adequately protected if evidence of course content or teacher preparation is needed.

Distribute the syllabus the first day of class and take time to discuss the syllabus and any additional details. In fact, it is a good practice to review the syllabus on the second class meeting, noting the importance of the activities, assignments, and objectives, and address any student questions. The importance of the syllabus to students can best be exemplified by a recent experience of the author while teaching a summer class. Before the second class session I was approached by a student, who had missed the first session, with a request for a copy of my syllabus and course outline—a sign of the rising expectations of students.

A good syllabus requires considerable work initially but minimal time in subsequent updates. Work put into the development of the syllabus will pay dividends. A syllabus is a scientific document and a work of art, and it should be shown that respect in its development and use.

Figure 4.2 is one of numerous syllabi formats that may be used. In some institutions the syllabus format is rigid and faculty are expected to adhere to it. In other situations faculty are permitted the flexibility of developing their own format as long as it is complete and specifies student requirements. In some situations the course outline may be included as part of the syllabus rather than as a separate document. Other items that may be included are: required materials, assignments, course philosophy, and classroom assessment procedures (Bianco-Mathis, 1996).

Another style of syllabus construction emphasizes three major parts. They are: the general course and instructor information, the specific course requirements, and college policies. Specific course requirements may include a listing of all required materials, the course rationale, course learning outcomes, assessment, and a brief summary of instructional methods. Under "college policies," important information needs to be included such as registration policy, student withdrawal policy, inclement weather policy and fees and refunds and well as term calendar (Stephan, 2000).

## Figure 4.2—Sample Course Syllabus

Achievement University
Syllabus
Name of Course: English 101-33241
Instructor: Dr. Dennis
Office: B151
Phone: 987-5037 (Office)
dgabrie@ ibm5060.ccc.edu (Internet address)
fax 987-5050
Office Hours: M-F 9:00 to 10:00
M,W, F: 12:00 to 2:00 (by appointment)
Lecture hours: 3
Lab hours: 0

**Class requirements:**
All papers must be typed or written on a word processor. Papers may be revised for a higher grade. Use the MLA format for all papers. Plan to spend three to four hours each week in the computer lab.

**Course description** (per catalog): Study and practice in the principles of good writing.

**Performance objectives:**
1. The student will organize and clarify the principles of basic written communication.
2. The student will complete critical readings as a basis for completion of his/her writing.
3. The student will develop and increase skills in expository and argumentative writing.

**Essay patterns:**
    Narrative
    Expository (analysis, contrast, cause-effect)
    Argument

**Schedule:**
January
10  Introduction to the course
    Diagnostic essay
    Homework: read chs. 1, 2. (handbook)
17  Discuss essay patterns, Ch. 2
    Return diagnostic essay w/ comments
    Discuss essay 1: narrative
    Hmwk: read Ch. 3
24  Discuss subordination, Ch. 3
    Discuss variety and details, Ch. 3
    assign essay 2
    Essay 1 due
    Hmwk: Ch. 4

31　Discuss writing the introduction, conclusion Ch. 4
　　Crash Course in Phonics: Punctuation (handout)
　　Discuss essay 2
　　Hmwk: Ch. 5

February

7　Subject and verb agreement
　　Usage problems
　　Essay 2 due
　　Hmwk: Ch. 6

14　Support paragraphs
　　Developing topics
　　Assign essay 3
　　Hmwk: Ch. 7

21　Using the exact word
　　Punctuation problems
　　Essay 3 due

28　Pronoun and antecedent
　　Usage problems
　　Assign essay 4
　　Hmwk: Ch. 9

March

7　Writing a paper for a literature class
　　Essay 4 due
　　Writing across the curriculum
　　Hmwk: Ch. 10

14　Discuss topic for final exam
　　Review course goals, objectives
　　Hmwk: Outline final exam

Textbooks: *The Compact Handbook*
　　　　　*American Heritage Dictionary, 3e*
　　Supplemental materials: 3.5" HD disk
　　Suggested daily/weekly readings: *New York Times*
　　　　　　　　　　　　　　　*Newsweek* magazine
　　　　　　　　　　　　　　　*Wall Street Journal*

Last day to drop class: 4 March

**Attendance policy:** Attendance in class is important. To that end, quizzes may NOT be made up.

**Final grade:** Quizzes　　　　　20% (one per week)
　　　　Essay 1　　　10% (due 1/24)
　　　　Essay 2　　　20% (due 2/7)
　　　　Essay 3　　　20% (due 2/21)
　　　　Essay 4　　　10% (due 3/7)
　　　　Final exam　　　20% (3/21, 8 to 10 AM)

## The Lesson Plan

A lesson plan is a must for all teachers because it acts as a reference and guide for each class meeting. A flexible lesson plan allows for discussion of appropriate current events and and provides a backup system if multimedia materials or equipment do not arrive or suffer a mechanical or electrical malfunction. The plan contains important questions and quotes from supplemental material not contained in the text, and should include definitions, comments on the purposes of the class, and student and teacher activities.

Make every effort to have lesson plans reflect your creative endeavors and unique abilities as a teacher. Often, the syllabus and to some extent the course outline are dictated to faculty. The demands for accountability and institutional goals sometimes restrict these two documents. Lesson plans, however, allow greatee flexibility and permit techniques and strategies unique to the instructor, including appropriate personal experiences and anecdotes.

After determining your objectives, you then outline the major topics that will be covered, including definitions and references to sources not in the textbook, in your daily lesson plans. Your lesson plan may include everything you need to take to the classroom such as notes, handouts, computer disks, software references, etc. (Stephan, 2000). Shown in figures 4.3 and 4.4 are examples of a lesson plan and a sample form. An effective method of planning a course is to construct a plan for each class meeting, number the lessons, place them in a loose-leaf binder, and maintain them as a record and a guide for activities.

Figure 4.3—Sample Lesson Plan

Course # and Name: Algebra 101
Date_____
Session #9
**Class Objectives:**
1. To demonstrate equations through the use of various expressions of equality
2. To prove equality of expressions through technique of substitution
**Definitions:**
1. *Equation* is a statement that two expressions are equal
2. *Expression* is a mathematical statement
3. *Linear equation* is equation of 1st order
**Student Activities:**
1. Complete sample problems in class
2. Demonstrate competence of sample by board work
**Instructor Activities:**
1. Demonstrate validity of solution of equations
2. Assure student understanding by personal observations by seat and board work
**Major Impact:**
Understand the solution of basic linear equations.
**Assignment:** Problems—Exercise 8, pp. 41-42.

Figure 4.4—Suggested Lesson Plan Format

Course number and Name_____Date_____
(after first page simply number chronologically)
Session #_____
Definitions to be covered_____
_____
Class objective(s)_____
_____
Student activities or exercises_____
_____
Instructor activities_____
_____
Major impact or thought_____
Assignment_____
_____

# CHAPTER 5
## TEACHING TECHNIQUES, INSTRUCTIONAL AIDS, TESTING

Once you have made the decision concerning your objectives for the course, the next step is to choose the instructional methods and strategies necessary to carry them out. In examining these teaching strategies and techniques, you should ask yourself the following questions:

- When should I teach by demonstration and when should I encourage students to try it themselves?

- When should I explain important topics and issues verbally and when should I prepare handouts for discussion?

- When should I lecture and when should I use question-and-answer strategies?

- When should I use audiovisual aids to support my points in discussion and lecture?

- When should I utilize multimedia technology and associated strategies to enhance my teaching?

In this chapter we will discuss some of the more common techniques, teaching aids, and evaluation procedures utilized in today's classrooms. These techniques, although not necessarily new or innovative, have proven valuable over the years to successful teachers. By utilizing a variety of teaching techniques, instructors can vary their students' learning experiences and generate excitement in the classroom.

## Teaching Techniques

Successful teaching depends to a certain degree upon the initiative, creativity, and risk-taking prowess of the instructor. Even instructors with these characteristics, however, must use a variety of techniques and approaches to be successful. Some of the more common techniques used by successful teachers include:

| Instructor-Based Techniques | Student-Based Techniques |
|---|---|
| Lectures | Active Learning |
| Class Discussions | Collaborative learning |
| Question/answer sessions | Role playing |
| Demonstrations | Buzz groups |
| Guest Lecturers | Student panels |
| Quality Control Circles | Oral reports/group projects |
| | Lab assignments |
| | Learning Cells |

### Out-of-Class Activities

Field trips/Site Visits
Journal/publication readings
Term papers/Research projects
Outside assignments
Case studies
Internet research

| Traditional Instructional Aids | Technology-Driven Aids |
|---|---|
| Handouts | Videos/films |
| Chalkboards/Whiteboards | Overhead projection |
| Flipcharts | Computer projection |
| Lecture Notes | Multimedia presentations |

These are but some of the possible activities to facilitate classroom instruction. You might start by checking off those techniques that you have used then go on to the more detailed descriptions of these classroom activities.

## Instructor-Based Techniques
### *The Lecture*

Extensive preparation and refinement are required to present a successful lecture. Although the lecture has long been recognized as one of the more appropriate ways to convey information, there is often a fine line between "telling" students and "presenting" a lecture. Historically, the lecture was intended for highly motivated and informed listeners who attended to hear a specific topic discussed. Today it has been adapted to nearly every classroom situation. The modern lecture frequently involves the integration of technology and other activities to form a total presentation.

A good lecture contribute the following to any teaching situation:

1. Lectures convey large amounts of information in a short period of time.
2. Lectures develop student interest in a subject.
3. Lectures maximize instructor control over the material and procedures.
4. Lectures present up-to-date facts not available in the text or other course materials.
5. Due to their passive nature, lectures cause minimum anxiety to students.

On the other hand, some of these advantages can lead to the disadvantages inherent in lecturing. They are:

1. Lectures place students in a passive and nonparticipative role.
2. Lectures assume that all students are learning and listening at the same pace and competency level.
3. Lectures do not normally contribute to higher levels of learning such as application, analysis, and synthesis.
4. Lectures can obstruct effective student feedback, especially in large classes.
5. Lecture material retention rates are significantly lower than other teaching techniques.

Listed below are several suggestions for building a successful lecture:

- Plan an expansive introduction of the lecture which encompasses the purpose of the lecture, the statement or series of questions which will be addressed, possibly an anecdote concerning the purpose of the lecture, and problems to be addressed.

- Take a few moments to research and analyze your class prior to the introduction. With the diversity of ages and backgrounds of the students of today, it is important that the lecture considers the recipients' status.

- In addition to course objectives, have specific objectives identified to yourself for the lecture.

- Do not read/refer to notes.

- Do not read from the text.

- Over-prepare. It will enhance your confidence.

- Use gestures. Remember a palm up is positive and down is negative.

- Encourage students to interrupt.

- Assist students in taking notes. Provide outlines and/or pause for note taking.

- Document references verbally, giving students time to write down the reference information and guide them to the reference documents.

- Prepare anecdotes and questions.

- Don't depend upon memory, write it down.

- Move around. Don't stand in one place or behind a lectern.

- Tell them what you are going to tell them, tell them, then tell them what you told them.

- Refer to examples or other topics.

- Tell them at the start what your intentions are and when you are changing topics.

- Summarize—it is important that the lecture be summarized, reviewing the main points and outlining the progress made from the beginning of the lecture to the end. Restate your expectations of what the students have gained from the day's session.

*Lecture Techniques.* Studies have shown that students retain more of the material presented in the early part of the lecture and less in the later phases. Thus, it is important that significant points are made early and then reinforced by activity later in the presentation. There are several methods to improve lectures. Adequate preparation with appropriate support of references, anecdotes, and handouts will enhance the effectiveness of the lecture. Depending upon memory for such support may prove ineffective; therefore, references, etc., should be written as part of the lecture notes. Physical appearance is also important, a business-like approach and dress will pay off while an unkempt appearance will negate hours of diligent preparation. Cue the class to the major points to be stressed in the presentation. Allow students time to take notes. Provide a complete summary with repetition and reinforcement of important points. It is important that vocabulary and definitions be explained. Avoid buzz words and jargon. Use the chalkboard and other visual techniques as necessary.

---

*A lecture does not mean that only the instructor talks. It is important that time be allowed during the lecture for student feedback, questions, and discussions.*

---

There are general guidelines to keep in mind when presenting the lecture. Although they are basic and well known, they are worth repeating here.

- Make certain your lecture is organized and presented in an orderly manner. Too often students are critical of instructors who appear to be rambling.

- Using illustrations throughout the lecture is an indication of a well organized lecture which the presenter is taking seriously.

- It is important that you remember to speak clearly and directly to the audience.

- Give mental breaks every ten minutes or so; that is, change the procedure by using an anecdote or activity so that the lecture is not a continuous one-way dialog.

- If you have a tendency to use distracters or mannerisms such as "you know" or "OK", be aware and avoid them.

- Use the chalk board, overhead, or any prop that you feel appropriate to enhance your lecture.

- Finally, do not hesitate to build "thinking pauses" into your lectures so your students have time mentally to catch their breath.

### Discussion

Discussions are important to any interactive learning environment. They help students to formulate logic in understanding and lead to higher order learning. They allow students to identify problems and to use other members of the group as resources. This is especially important in today's diverse classroom, where older experienced adults and younger students will be sitting side by side in your class.

When stimulating class discussions, you quickly realize that this must be planned the same as any other classroom activity. Too often there is the tendency to "wait for the discussion to happen". This often leads to a lack of discussion or discussions that are not related to the topic at hand. One discussion technique is to start with a common experience. The experience might be a current event, a common problem to be solved, or a controversial issue. It may be necessary to place students in small groups, give them a topic, and have them find a solution or develop a hypothesis. Then each group can interact and question each other's findings.

Preparation for a full-class discussion requires planning as well as review of the day's topics. If the topic has been discussed with your previous classes, draw from that experience or even give some of the previous classes' conclusions and have the present class react to them. When leading the discussion, give all students the opportunity to speak. If one or two students monopolize the discussion you may wish to take their comments and ask the rest of the class to respond to them.

If there is a lull in the discussion, sometimes it is best to let the silence continue for awhile; usually there are students in the class that will feel a need to break the silence.

Urge students to talk to each other and not to you, the instructor, and if there are students who do not participate, be cognizant of that and ask them to respond to other student's comments. In leading discussions, more than any other situation in the interactive classroom, you must remember that you are a facilitator of learning and not the director of learning.

### Question/Answer

Questioning students is an important tool for stimulating classroom participation and motivating students. Experienced teachers make it a rule to question as many different students as possible during a class session. Besides encouraging student participation and arousing student curiosity, questioning students is an effective way to gauge their preparation for class as well as their progress and understanding of the class topic. Eliciting answers can develop student confidence in self-expression. The right kinds of questions can also encourage higher orders of learning such as analysis, synthesis, and evaluation.

There is hardly a disadvantage associated with questioning if good judgment is exercised. Appropriate timing is important—pace questions so students have time to phrase their answers. For example, it would be unkind to continue to question a student who is embarrassed or is having difficulty responding. Such students need to be "brought along" in the classroom.

---

Good questioning involves several strategies:

- *Use open-ended questions when possible, that is, do not use questions that have a yes/no answer.*

- *Use questions that elicit a comment or additional queries from students, even to the point of saying to a student, "What do you think of that?"*

- *Questions should be part of the lesson plan. Prepare them ahead of time—don't wait for them to "happen."*

---

Different types of questions have different purposes. They are usually found in four categories: knowledge, content, discussion, and stimulation. For example,

- a **knowledge question** might be: "What is a spreadsheet?"

- a **content question** might be: "What are the functions of a spreadsheet?"

- a **discussion question** might be: "What are the advantages and disadvantages of using a spreadsheet?"

- a **stimulation question** might be: "How can spreadsheets enhance your job accuracy?" This may be followed with "Why do you think this?"

One would not normally pose questions as a form of graded evaluation because this intimidates students and typically negates the purpose of asking the question. Whenever possible, questions should be addressed to individuals by name rather than to the whole class. If your class is giving you the silent treatment, a quick question and answer can bail you out.

Another benefit to using questions and answers is the way it encourages students to ask questions of their own. Skillful questioning stimulates students to respond with questions that show higher levels of thinking.

Encouraging student questioning means eliminating any threat to the questioner. Sometimes teachers, without knowing, discourage student questioning by moving so quickly through the course material that they don't appear to have time to consider a question. Some teachers may actually say "hold your questions until the end of class." This is not only discouraging; it also runs the risk that the student will forget a question valuable to the class discussion.

Some of the techniques involved in encouraging questions from students include:

- show complete respect for any questions or comments made by students,

- specifically ask students questions during the presentation,

- use probing questions with the students,

- ask students if they need clarification on any points or issues,

- ask students to give the pros and cons of a particular issue or point, and

- have other students ask questions concerning the response.

### *The Demonstration*

For classes that lend themselves to this technique, a demonstration is an effective way to teach skills because it combines hearing with seeing. Research shows that nearly 90 percent of learning takes place when both of these two senses are involved. Demonstration has other advantages:

- It is motivational.

- It attracts attention and can be presented to groups or to individual students.

- It is effective for large group instruction.

The demonstration is probably under-utilized as a teaching tool. To be successful, demonstration requires extensive preparation. To adequately prepare, you should simulate the demonstration prior to the class presentation. This allows you to examine the problems, be alert to possible difficulties, and even to forewarn the students that some steps are particularly difficult. Through this simple warning, the students will lend support and assist in making the demonstration successful.

Some guidelines for a successful demonstration include:

- Double-check that you have all materials and tools. (The most common flaw in classroom demonstrations is "something is missing.")

- Complete a checklist for materials and procedures as you perform the demonstration. Students can then "check" to assure correct procedure.

- State and distribute the objectives of the demonstration along with the expected outcomes.

- Have students write conclusions to the demonstration.

Although demonstrations carry the risk of failure; this is a small risk as compared to the benefits gained by showing as well as telling. Students normally will be less critical of teachers who are not successful when attempting complicated techniques. They are much more critical of boring repetitious classes.

### The Guest Lecturer

In most college classrooms, guest lecturers are under-utilized. Most communities are rich with individuals who are willing, usually at no charge, to share their experiences and expertise. Our rapidly changing world makes it nearly impossible for faculty members to remain current on all issues. Inviting individuals who are on the cutting edge of changes in business, industry and community agencies to speak not only provides information but also a glimpse of the "real world" of work. Again, it is necessary to structure such a visitation so that students are aware of the objectives of the activity.

Beware of the danger that students will become a listening audience rather than questioning participants; students need to either prepare questions prior to the visit or be given time after the guest lecturer speaks to compose questions. You should also be sure to brief the guest lecturer on the objectives and intent of the visit and to act as mediator between students and lecturer.

### Quality Control Circles

Quality control circles are one of the most dynamic and interesting concepts that has evolved in the past decade. It is a management technique generally credited to the Japanese (Weimer, 1990). This technique can be very effective with adult students because it requires the involvement of employees (students) in some of the class decision-making activities. It is a relatively simple process and is especially helpful for part-time teachers who do not have daily contact with students.

During the first class session, the instructor asks for five or six volunteers to join the quality circle. The group meets periodically with the instructor, possibly during a class break or after class, to provide feedback concerning the progress of the class. The feedback might include comments concerning lecture, discussion, homework, testing, or other class activities. This process provides an ongoing feedback mechanism that involves students. It will also provide student support as you implement the circles' suggestions in the class presentation.

## Student-Based Techniques
### *Active Learning*

If you have recently read professional literature or attended faculty development workshops, you have heard the expression "active learning." You may wonder, is this strategy significantly different from learning strategies of the past? Basically, active student learning dictates that the personal learning needs of the students override the instructor/discipline-oriented learning of the past. In this scenario, the teacher develops a learning environment where students actively talk, listen and react to the course content through group activities, role playing, cooperative learning, and other student interaction techniques. The purpose of these activities is for students to apply what they are learning by sharing.

In active learning, students are no longer passive participants but become responsible for their own learning. This provides students opportunities to collaborate and cooperate with others, rather than competing. Critical thinking skills are emphasized as well as an increased opportunity for students to express their values and understanding of their culture.

As you consider these interactive student-centered techniques, you may be tempted to ask, "don't all teachers do these things?" The answer is no; regardless of the emphasis placed upon varying teaching techniques and student involvement, studies still show that the teacher does over 60 percent of the talking in class.

Active learning techniques are applicable for all disciplines. In implementing these techniques it is important to recognize that the instructor's role is as a facilitator rather than as a director of learning. The instructor as a facilitator must establish rapport with the class and encourage and stimulate student discussion. Treating students with respect and showing a sense of humor and patience will help to establish this kind of environment. Students need to understand that their questions and comments are valuable and that they will not be ridiculed for seemingly inappropriate observations or questions.

> Very often nonverbal cues can be used by the instructor to relax the students. Talking directly to and walking toward the students who are raising questions or issues shows the entire class you respect them. A nod of the head or a concentrated look conveys a similar message that you are interested or understand. Moving around the room, looking relaxed and actually joining the class is another valuable nonverbal activity.

### Cooperative/Collaborative Learning

Cooperative learning (also called collaborative learning), is one of the oldest educational techniques. In theory, cooperative learning brings students with differing abilities together into small groups where they teach each other the concepts of the class by reinforcing lecture and text materials. In practice, students either work on specific projects cooperatively or take selected quizzes and/or tests together. The process forces all students to become actively involved in classroom activities. Adult learners relate to cooperation in the classroom because of the cooperation required in most workplaces.

To effectively use cooperative learning techniques, you must spend considerable time structuring the situation so that each student understands their role as well as the objectives of the group.

A good cooperative learning group needs several conditions, that:

- all students must participate,

- a method to capture the individual member participation be used, and

- a written product must be the result.

For instructors, the two basic requirements for cooperative learning are thorough planning and a total commitment.

As a facilitator the instructor becomes an idea person, a resource person, a mediator (conflict resolution is as much an accomplishment in cooperative education as it is in the workplace or in life itself), and a supporter of students' efforts. Virtually all academic and technical disciplines can benefit from this technique.

Preliminary planning includes a discussion of classroom goals, specific activities that can be assigned cooperatively, and the balance sought between traditional and cooperative classroom activities. If grades are going to be assigned for group work the students must be made aware of this at the beginning of the term; the assignment of the same grade to each member of a group is the incentive needed to make cooperative learning work effectively.

The optimum size for a work group is four or five students; more students can be unwieldy while fewer opens the door to domineering students. Groups can be formed by:

- students themselves,

- the instructor assigning students to a group,

- random assignment, or

- selection based upon similar interests or specific criteria.

Typically, instructors should assign students, rather than allowing to form their own groups.

Decided disadvantages of student-based selection are that students may choose to be with friends, thus excluding assimilation of new students into the mainstream of the class, and there may be stress in arranging groups if students do not know each other and have no basis for selection.

The benefits of cooperative learning include: adults have a vehicle to get to know others in class; attendance tends to be better (a result of a commitment to the group); improved grades due to an increased understanding of the subject matter; classroom groups lead to study groups outside of class; and students become participants in their own learning.

Instructors must regularly re-evaluate their classroom styles to accommodate changes in technology, abilities of students, and demands of students. Cooperative learning is but one of many viable strategies to encourage participation by students. Obstacles that might be encountered are: some students feel they have paid money to take the course, therefore the teacher is expected to stand in front of the class and lecture; groups may not take an assignment seriously; and some individuals may have difficulty working within a group. However, problems can be overcome by involving students in decisions regarding cooperative activities and adapting the assignments to the students in the class.

Adults are sensitive to how others view them and tend to be more candid when working in small groups; working with fellow students provides adults the opportunity to grow within the small group until they are ready to face larger groups (Sego, 1996).

### The Student Panel

A student panel can be used as an alternative to lecturing by giving groups of students the opportunity to do the presenting. However, it must be structured so the specific objectives of the assignment are clearly defined prior to the panel presentation. Normally, a panel should consist of two to four members. Each member of the panel should be assigned specific topics or issues to be presented and/or defended. After the presentation, the rest of the class should be divided into discussion groups so these students can define their positions on the panel's topic. Instructors should remember to help students in developing open-ended questions for the rest of the class. A carefully structured panel is a valuable learning experience for the participants as well as the class.

### The Learning Cell

In learning cells, students work in pairs to help each other learn; typically, the entire class is paired off for this activity. The pairs can work together in many different ways. It may involve an reading assignment in which the students share what they have read and then develop questions to present to one another. In this case they are demonstrating their reading comprehension and understanding of the issues while sharing their responses. Another possibility uses an open-question format where students can exercise their creativity in their responses or in a problem-solving situation. During the process the teacher moves about the room, going from pair to pair, seeking feedback and answering questions. Learning cells may be term-long assignments of students in pairs or may be assigned for a single class meeting.

### Buzz Groups

As an in-class activity, the buzz group's purpose is to solve a specific problem or compare and contrast an issue. The instructor identifies the discussion topic or problem and allows students to form small groups, usually of three to five students. The students are given the freedom to develop their own discussion guidelines for reaching a solution to the issue. The solution is prepared for presentation, possibly on a flipchart or overhead transparency for the following class session. Occasionally the instructor may have a solution prepared and use it as a discussion of the differences between the student buzz groups' and the instructor's conclusions.

 Buzz groups should not be confused with small group projects. Buzz groups are as a quick conclusion activity that takes 10 to 15 minutes of class time.

## Out-of-Class Activities

### *Outside Readings/Written Assignments*

Outside readings and additional assignments can be used by part-time instructors in several ways. Since neither the instructor nor the student is on campus for extensive library use, outside readings and references should be listed in the syllabus. It will aid part-time students significantly if materials and periodicals selected are available in public libraries or on the Internet. The preparation of handouts with reference numbers will also assist students. This allows students to spend their time in the library actually using the materials rather than searching for them. Again, being specific in terms of the topic and objectives (and points counted toward the grade) are necessary for a successful outside reading assignment.

### *The Project*

Student projects are one-way students can get the opportunity to learn outside the classroom. Projects may consist of in-depth research into a class topic or a community-based activity such as agency visitations, interviews, or case studies. A properly developed project should allow students to choose from a variety of related activities within their own sphere of interest. After topics are selected, instructor expectations for completion of the project should be clarified. The project should weigh significantly in the final evaluation and assignment of a grade.

### *The Case Study*

Traditionally, case studies have been used mainly in sociology or psychology classes. The case study may, however, be used in many other disciplines. Students may be given case studies of individuals or processes in finance, investing, historic contrast, geology or other class situations. In a good case study, the instructor establishes the scenario, the objectives of the case, and the problem(s) that may be encountered. Students may then be given time to read and research the project and write their case paper or make an oral presentation which can result in student discussions to reach consensus or a conclusion. Case studies are normally assigned to individual students and not to groups.

### Field Trips

Field trips should be planned so that the entire session of the field trip is on location. The class activities and trip objectives should be outlined prior to the trip. Arrange the class in small groups, specify to the students what they are to observe. At the conclusion of the visit, meet to discuss the major points observed and any conclusions to be made. The most effective field trips include credit toward the grade and require a written or oral report.

### Large Group Instruction

Although not a specific classroom technique, there are several strategies to improve large group instruction. Large classes are more impersonal and usually more difficult to teach. Successful large classes require greater preparation of materials, including more handouts and visual aids. The importance of a well-prepared lecture takes on added importance in large group instruction.

Some suggestions for easing the burden of teaching large classes include:

- **start out positively** by indicating that although large, the class is important and you are glad to be there;
- **keep a seating chart;**
- **try to learn a few student's names each day,** walk around the large classroom and try to identify students with whom you have had discussions;
- **use techniques such as buzz groups, panels, collaborative learning**—don't assume that standard strategies do not work;

- **utilize the cell or partner format.** In a class of 100, utilizing cells reduces responses to 50, or utilize cooperative learning strategies. Again, in a class of 100, using this technique will reduce the class to the equivalent of 20 students;

- **share your research, anecdotes, and background.** With a large class, chances are that someone in your class may have had similar experiences and might be willing to share them;

- **utilize the overhead projector, videos, and all types of technology** to vary the teaching activities;

- **use modern technology to communicate with your students.** Use your e-mail to share pertinent questions with all students. Or create a chatroom, bulletin board, or listserv. Be sure to share the responses with the rest of your class;

- **involve students** by asking for a show of hands or holding up colored cards (green for "I understand," red for "I don't understand");

- **have students write a brief response** paragraph to major questions and have them hand it in;

- **at the end of class ask students to drop a written question** to you on the way out, and at the beginning of the next class use the question to commence discussions;

- **keep students involved by giving short quizzes** (maybe ungraded) and use a show of hands to get feedback on the correct responses;

- **clearly identify major points and questions;**

- **arrange a 20-minute discussion group** before and/or after class for students who are having trouble in a large group setting; and

- **move around**—up the aisles and around the room as you lecture.

It is important that active techniques be utilized in large classes. Many teachers have a tendency to "give up" the interactive student responses, thinking that it is impossible in large group instruction.

## Instructional Aids

Modern technology has opened a new vista of tools for use in the modern classroom. The comphrensive multimedia presentation requiring considerable training and support materials such as computer hardware and software is described in greater detail in Chapter 6. A brief review of the traditional instructional aids is contained herein.

### Overhead Transparencies

The overhead projector has become one of the most popular support tools in education because it allows instructors to face the class while showing images on the screen using normal room lighting. Overhead projectors are inexpensive and are usually readily available from the academic division office or the audio-visual department. Some projectors are equipped with a roll that provides a continuous writing surface. This enables the retention of information on the roll in the event students later wish to discuss specific points and is especially useful in mathematics, engineering, etc. classes.

There is no limit to the artistic excellence that can be produced on a transparency. Many faculty members easily prepare their own transparencies. Transparencies may be typewritten, handwritten, computer-generated, or drawn on standard-size plain white paper and instantaneously produced on a standard copier. Many times it is worth the extra effort to make a professional-looking overhead transparency. They are easily maintained, durable, and thus can be a permanent part of future presentations.

### Videotape

Probably the most effective modern instructional aid is the videotape. With the reduction in cost of camcorders and tape itself, the possibilities for expanded use are nearly endless. Most institutions now have equipment for instructors who wish to develop their own video clips as well as a library of tapes that may be applicable to your class. Videos are not only attention getters, but provide the opportunity for direct student involvement when students produce their own videos. However, instructors must indicate to the students the objectives behind any videos and combine the video with discussion, a written report, or other activity.

### Flipchart

A commonly used visual aid for business seminars is a simple flipchart. When adapted to the classroom, the flipchart has many advantages over a chalkboard or overhead projector. The flipchart, a large tablet with pages that can be flipped vertically, is especially useful for small groups to record their discussions and conclusions. Instructors can record major points of a presentation and have room to add notes, descriptions, or comments. The information can then be retained by tearing off the page and taping it to the wall for future reference. A flipchart and felt-tip pen can be one of the most effective tools in the active classroom.

 NOTE: When planning on an instructional aid, be sure you have all the equipment you require before the class begins whether it's chalk, markers, flipchart easels, masking tape, or the TV/VCR to show your tape.

### Handouts

Although sometimes overused in the past, handouts are still a valuable instrument for instructors. Modern copy technology along with computers and printers make preparing and updating easy. Handouts should be used for material that students will need for reference, such as important definitions, computations, or position statements for discussion. Handouts for lecture purposes should contain only an outline of the material discussed with space for students to add their own comments.

A serious note of caution: be careful of copyright violations! Your supervisor or department head should be able to provide you with the Fair Use guidelines you will need to follow.

## Tests and Testing

There are multiple reasons for testing students. First and foremost is the evaluation to assist in the assignment for the total grade. In addition, however, tests serve multiple purposes. Testing communicates to the instructor if the course objectives are being met and to what degree. Of equal importance, tests are used as an instructional tool and a learning device for students. When tests are used for evaluation you must be careful to inform the students at the beginning of the class of the testing procedure, when they will be given, and the criteria upon which they will be based. Too often students are overheard criticizing their instructors with, "they didn't test over what they talked about in class."

## Test/Question Types

The major types of tests used in college classes are: essay, multiple-choice, and recall. In special circumstances, performance, oral, and short answer tests may also be utilized.

*Essay Tests/Questions.* Essay tests are still one of the most popular of colleges tests. They are effective at any level of the learning hierarchy. Although essay tests require considerable time for students to respond, they do give an in-depth perspective of overall student ability. There are several factors to remember when writing test questions that require essay answers. Most important is that essay questions should be related to the written course objectives. They should incorporate a significant amount of content, including discussion, contrasting, comparing, etc. Finally, you must be certain that in terms of vocabulary, content, and subject covered, the student has sufficient background to respond adequately to the question being asked and that the question is not ambiguous or deceptive.

Grading essay questions presents the greatest problem. You must keep in mind that essay questions are asking students to be objective, yet justify their answers. The appropriate way to judge an essay response is to list important items for the response and prioritize them, assigning more points to the highest priority. Assigning points to the prioritized criteria will then lead to a degree of grading objectivity.

 You must be cautious, however, that essay questions do not ask for student opinions since it's impossible to assign evaluation points to opinions.

*Multiple-choice Tests/Questions.* With the advent of computerized scoring and large classes, multiple-choice tests probably are the most used tests in college classrooms today. They not only are efficient in terms of time consumed, but with the use of item analysis, can determine question validity.

The development of multiple-choice questions is not a simple matter. The actual construction of the multiple-choice tests has several general guidelines, including:

- do not include answers that are obviously correct or incorrect, including impossible responses or distracters,
- be sure the correct answers are scattered throughout the response mechanism,
- provide four possible responses to minimize the guess factor,
- do not use "all of the above" or "none of the above,"
- do not use the terms never, always, likely, or similar adjectives that may divert the meaning for the student,
- be consistent with the format so that students are not confused with wording or punctuation changes, and
- keep choices approximately the same length since incorrect answers are frequently shorter than correct ones.

Disadvantages of multiple-choice tests are: they often test on only the knowledge level rather analysis and synthesis; they provide opportunity for guessing; and they depend primarily on recall and memory.

*Recall and Completion Tests/Questions.* Recall items may be posed as simple questions, completion, or brief response. Used too often, these tests tend to encourage students to memorize rather than understand. There are, however, advantages to recall tests. They are relatively simple to grade and construct; they can address a broad field of content; and they require specific recall rather than guessing or rationalization.

Some suggestions for developing recall questions are:
- Give information concerning the answer prior to the answer blank,
- Qualify information so students are clear about the response,
- Include responses at the analysis and synthesis level,
- Pose questions so that only one correct response is usable,
- Allow sufficient and equal space for the response,
- Avoid patterns of responses,
- Avoid direct quotes, and
- Avoid specific descriptors or adjectives.

 True/false questions are not commonly used at the college level any longer. Although they may have their place in a sampling of student responses or learning activity, they generally are not accepted as being objective or valid.

## Assigning Grades
### The Basics

Grading students is probably the most difficult task for faculty. All of the elements of teaching (preparation, presentation, and student activity) are reflected in the grading process. In addition, in an era of accountability, teachers are sometimes called upon to justify grades with documentation. Thus the establishment of firm criteria for grading is necessary. There are some general rules that are helpful in establishing the grading process. They are as follows:

- Communicate criteria clearly to the students.
- Include criteria other than test scores.
- Avoid irrelevant factors such as attendance and tardiness in the grading criteria.
- Place grading criteria carefully throughout the course.
- Weigh grading criteria carefully and always have a plan.
- Grade students on their achievement.

Many years ago, teachers used the technique of "grading on the curve." This placed students in competition with each other rather than cooperating in the learning experience. The practice has been abandoned in the modern classroom.

### Evaluation Plan

In order to clearly delineate criteria for assignment of grades, it is helpful if you first develop an evaluation plan. An evaluation plan is a very simple device developed in a short worksheet form. The plan contains all of the factors that apply to the evaluation of the students. Across from these factors is listed a percentage of weight that will be assigned to various factors. A third column indicates the points received for each factor. A sample plan is shown in the figure 5.1 below.

### Figure 5.1—Evaluation Chart

| Grade Factors | Percentage of Final Grade | Possible Points | Points Received |
|---|---|---|---|
| Tests | 60% | 90 | _____ |
| Paper | 20% | 30 | _____ |
| Project | 10% | 10 | _____ |
| Class Participation | 10% | 15 | _____ |
| TOTALS | 100% | 150 | _____ |

Note that this type of plan allows you the freedom to assign any number of points to any criteria or activity because the final percentage will always come out to 100 percent.

 This documentation clearly indicates to the students the process by which evaluation is conducted in a businesslike and professional manner. Once the evaluation plan is completed, it is essential that it be included in the course syllabus since that is the official document of the course.

# CHAPTER 6
## TEACHING AND LEARNING WITH TECHNOLOGY

*This chapter is contributed by Gary Wheeler. We are grateful to him for sharing his expertise about educational technology and it applications for adjunct faculty. Gary Wheeler is the Associate Executive Director, Miami University, Middletown Campus, Ohio.*

### Introduction

Over the past decade educators have seen the increasing use of various kinds of technology in the college classroom with an accompanying challenge for appropriate and effective instruction. Technology that first was used in business and industry is now commonplace in the classroom. In much the way that overhead projectors were first used to great impact displaying individual scores in bowling alleys before being used to display text and charts to students during class, business productivity software is being adapted to the needs of education. Beyond word processing, commonly used computer software includes communication software (from simple e-mail to course management systems) and presentation software. There is so much data available via electronic networks that educators desperately need the ability to search for and find relevant information. The purpose of this chapter is to introduce instructors to what they need to know about these technologies and to provide tips on effective strategies to enhance student learning.

A widely used set of guidelines for classroom practice, "Seven Principles for Good Practice in Undergraduate Education," was published in the March 1987 issue of the *American Association for Higher Education Bulletin*. In 1997 authors Art Chickering and Steve

Ehrmann updated their seven principles with suggestions for using technology to enhance the original principles (Chickering & Ehrmann, 1997). Below are paraphrases of some of their arguments with particular application suggestions for the adjunct/part-time faculty member, following each of the seven principles:

1. **Good practice encourages contacts between students and faculty.**

   The use of electronic communications can provide an additional opportunity for students and faculty to contact each other. The opportunity to connect with and get to know a faculty member well helps a student make personal connections to the subject matter and make personal commitments for improved classroom behaviors and practices. Some students may find it easier to discuss individual responses to the academic material or to ask questions using a form of contact that is not face-to-face. Resources may be shared and distributed among the members of the class. Faculty may be able to offer additional assistance to students or provide a forum for discussion. Virtual office hours may be provided.

   *The part-time faculty member is often one who does not have an office on campus or may not hold regular office hours beyond speaking with students immediately before or after classes. Their own time constraints make it difficult for them to spend much out-of-class time with students. Electronic communications technologies can provide a useful vehicle for part-time faculty to increase their contact with students effectively and efficiently.*

2. **Good practice develops reciprocity and cooperation among students.**

   Student learning is improved and deepened when individuals work with and collaborate with others. Education is a social activity.

Among the skills most valued by business and industry is the ability to work as a member of a team. Similar to improved student/faculty contact leading to better student performance, it also is clear that student learning is improved and deepened by effective student interaction.

The use of technology, from groupware and e-mail to classroom management systems, provides a mechanism for increased interaction among students. Collaborative learning can be fostered by the use of existing technologies.

*The issues for the part-time faculty regarding how to best promote student teamwork and collaboration center around having enough time in which to do team-based work and finding effective ways to encourage interaction while maintaining appropriate levels of classroom control. Technology provides effective solutions to both of these concerns.*

3.  **Good practice uses active learning techniques.**

    The commonly heard concern about the use of technology in the classroom—that it encourages passive learning by students—is more an issue related to the appropriate use of classroom strategies. There are many technologies that encourage active learning, from tools that feature learning by doing to real-time simulations to the incorporation of computer-based data in discovery science. The challenge is in helping faculty learn enough about the tools that encourage active learning and in encouraging them to employ active learning strategies in the classroom. Faculty teach by using a number of strategies, including lecture, use of textbooks and readings, discussions, practice exercises and activities, problem-solving and discovery-based work, field trips, and interactive opportunities. Technology can provide enrichment for each of these strategies.

*Good active learning practice ensures that students have opportunities for putting into practice some of the ideas and concepts presented in class. Find ways to get students moving (intellectually) by giving them responsibility for finding information, for evaluating its relevance, for synthesizing disparate pieces of information, and for using the materials of the class to solve real-world problems. One strategy for part-time faculty to engage students in active learning is having students participate in organizing information that will be presented. While there are many ways to do this, one mechanism has students work in groups, organizing and deciding on which pieces of information will be presented in class, how it will be presented, and what problems are being addressed by this information. The in-class presentation can be made by the instructor or by the students themselves.*

4. **Good practice gives prompt feedback.**

   Students need to recognize both what they know and what they do not—providing consistent and rapid feedback helps students by reinforcing correct knowledge and by pointing out where additional steps toward understanding need to be taken. There are many ways technology can provide appropriate feedback. These range from computer-based tutoring systems and simulations that give immediate responses to the use of e-mail to provide narrative feedback. Word processing programs can incorporate notations to student writing. Audio feedback can be sent as attachments e-mailed to students. Students can create electronic portfolios of their work, including their own self-assessments using text-based or audio/video systems and get feedback electronically from faculty and peers. Students can use e-mail to contact experts at distant sites for guidance and feedback.

   *The effective part-time faculty member will encourage multiple mechanisms for providing feedback to students throughout the course of study. Formative feedback can be enhanced by using technology to connect the student with peers, outside experts, and other faculty.*

5. **Good practice emphasizes time-on-task.**

   One of the more difficult tasks facing students today is time management. Making time to spend on class-related activities competes with time spent on employment, family responsibilities, commuting, recreation, and co-curricular or social activities among others. Technology enables students to work effectively whenever they choose using computer networks.

   The time when students have the most energy for work does not always coincide with the time scheduled for classes. Students can work as a member of a team without spending the time coordinating schedules and meeting face-to-face. Time-on-task can be greater when the time expectations for students (and faculty) are adapted realistically to the schedules of modern life.

   *The part-time faculty member can establish specific guidelines for time-on-task as well as the qualitative time students spend with each other studying or interacting as a member of a group or team. Once guidelines are established and expected outcomes described, students can document their time-on-task as a part of their own development or to indicate the level of involvement with a project.*

6. **Good practice communicates high expectations.**

   High levels of achievement come from high levels of expectation. It is good practice to use technology for communicating and embodying high expectations. Significant work can be accomplished by incorporating compelling real-life problems, demonstrating the complexities of varying perspectives, and collecting information from a wide range of original sources and conflicting sets of data. The criteria for interacting with and interpreting data can be communicated effectively and widely among students throughout the course using technology and can include multiple examples and case studies via websites and models.

*Part-time faculty members, whether teaching introductory or more advanced professional practice courses, should find ways to communicate their expectations and performance requirements using as many ways and modes of delivery as they do for course content. Simple declarations in class or in the syllabus are not enough. High expectations are communicated through how the classroom is managed, by the thoroughness of material presentation, and via the kinds of activities students are expected to accomplish. Technology provides a vehicle for regular reminders of expectations. It also can reinforce high expectations by enabling students to work with primary source materials and by providing a ready vehicle for demonstrating complex problems and solutions.*

7. **Good practice respects diverse talents and ways of learning.**

There is no one model for achieving excellence, based on modes of learning styles or personality types. Technology can enable self-paced learning; enriched projects for deeper understanding; multiple modes of expression that include data, audio, and video; and customized processes for student learning. While some percentage of students can do well while being instructed using the didactic model of the teacher lecturing, this model does not work for all—the typical lecture is not interactive nor does it encourage active learning or student reflection. It typically gives a single interpretation of materials and is more responsive to the perceived quality needs of the profession or discipline than the needs of the students who have diverse learning styles. Technology helps by enlarging the capabilities of all teachers by using presentation styles appropriate for the range of learning styles in today's classrooms.

*Use the available technology to search for information on student learning styles and to find out more about the students in the class. Looking at the websites of area high schools and communities can provide useful insights into the kinds of places that have produced your students. Examine the demographics of the area. Find out the level of students' technology use and their level of comfort with technology. One lesson that is regularly learned by the faculty member who uses electronic communication (e-mail) with students is that those students who are less likely to speak up in class are likely to communicate more vigorously using e-mail. Another lesson is that students who had difficulty understanding complex concepts when these were presented orally, often learn these same concepts more easily and deeply when the presentation mode is visual, interactive, and employs active learning strategies.*

## Communicating with Students

Communicating with students goes beyond the expected in-class activity of the faculty member telling information and eliciting responses. Strategies for promoting student learning need to include multiple means for effectively communicating with students. This communication needs to be a two-way interaction, enabling the instructor and students to share information, discuss ideas, and to evaluate together the issues being examined in the course.

Technology-based strategies for improving communication include the use of e-mail, bulletin boards, instant messaging, and chatrooms including those provided as a part of a course management system such as WebCT, (**http://www.Webct.com/**), or Blackboard (**http://www.blackboard.com/**). Both of these are widely used at American colleges and universities.

### Using e-mail

E-mail is used by virtually all students and faculty in higher education, although the particular software used by each institution may vary. Most operate similarly and begin with getting a user account (often including an e-mail address) on the institution's e-mail system, getting the appropriate software on office and home computers, and establishing the appropriate settings for communicating with others using this software. Some institutional e-mail systems use proprietary software while others have an open system, allowing anyone to interact with its members.

 The best advice for faculty and students: learn the processes at your campus for access to campus networks and software and take advantage of any campus-provided workshops for using critical software, whether operating and network systems or e-mail.

Once the faculty and students can successfully log on, gaining access to the campus or external (AOL or other Internet Service Provider) network services, the class communication processes and activities may proceed. Strategies for successful use of e-mail include the use of one-to-one e-mail correspondence or one-to-many e-mail distribution using groups or listservs.

One-to-one contact involves the instructor and student exchanging information, usually something that is specific to that student only, with the instructor, for example, responding to a question by this student or the student commenting on material presented during class. One-to-many contact enables an instructor (or student) to send the same e-mail message to a larger group—the instructor sending general information such as study questions to the entire class or a student sending their input to a class discussion. Various files such as word processed documents, audio, video files, or spreadsheets may be attached to e-mail messages.

 While attaching files is occasionally necessary, it is good practice to limit the use of attachments since attachments may be of a size and file type that make transmission and reading difficult.

One-to-many contact via e-mail is assisted by the creation of e-mail groups and listservs. Anyone may create within their e-mail software a group of people who together would receive particular e-mail messages. Usually this is done by creating a new named character or alias within the software's address book and, where the user would indicate the e-mail address of the person to whom the mail would be sent, including multiple e-mail addresses. The instructor might create an e-mail group that includes all of the members of the class. A student might create a group e-mail address that includes everyone in a study group or of several friends who get together for lunch on Wednesdays. The use of a group name with multiple e-mail addresses enable a single e-mail message to be sent easily to more than one person. When the number of people who could be a member of such an e-mail group gets fairly large—a good rule of thumb is any number larger than ten—a listserv would be helpful.

Listservs are created and maintained with software used by the institution's computer servers. The lists of people on a given server that automatically sends e-mail from one person to a whole group depends on how the lists are created. Lists may be created where individuals subscribe to the listserv (voluntary membership) or from a database of names and e-mails of individuals who are logically connected in some way (involuntary or automatic membership)—for example, everyone listed by the registrar as enrolled in a particular class.

Tips for getting the most out of using e-mail with students:

- **Make sure that all students have e-mail access and accounts before using e-mail as a primary mode of communication outside the classroom.** Many institutions automatically assign e-mail accounts when students register for classes, others require students to sign up for an account at some central location. Find out if your students have access to the Internet from home, dormitory/apartment, or some other location where they can receive e-mail messages. Also find out what the limitations are for your students' e-mail—they may not be able to receive or decipher attachments, particularly attachments over a certain size or unusual file types.

- **Establish processes and expectations for e-mail use by your students that include guidelines regarding tone of language, frequency, educational purpose, and format.** As a part of the class syllabus, indicate the class expectations for using e-mail. A good practice is providing a welcome e-mail to all students in the class that provides a model for how the e-mail communication will be conducted. The structure of the model e-mail should include a subject line and a description linked to the educational purpose of the e-mail discussion to let everyone know what is being said along with any other issues. (See the Figure 6.1.)

- **Let students know how often they are expected to contribute to the discussion.** It is common practice to have students be expected to contribute one original e-mail commentary per week during the academic term and to also contribute one e-mail that responds to one or more received e-mails.

- **Encourage student e-mails for discussion purposes and monitor the discussion but realize that you do not need to evaluate all student e-mail.** Don't think you need to respond to everything in every student e-mail. If you've set up a strong system for encouraging e-mail discussion, you won't be able to keep up and you are likely to get in the way of your students communicating with each other. It may be important for you to monitor the tone of the discussion and contribute by setting an example, but open dialogue can be hindered by too much heavy-handed control. Do not allow anonymous e-mail discussion—it is too easy to make strong comments without the responsibility for being civil when the sender is anonymous.

A popular form of almost instantaneous communication, similar to e-mail, is instant messaging. Using specialized software, similar to e-mail and usually connected to the Internet web browser, instant messaging enables a user to write a note which almost immediately will appear in a window on the recipient user's computer. This immediacy is popular with many students because it provides an environment for "talking" to others that is similar to using the telephone. Because of its immediacy, instant messaging is difficult to control in an educational environment. On the other hand, it may provide exactly the right kind of contact between students who are studying for exams and who want the benefits of studying together despite being in two different places. Be clear about the circumstances in which instant messaging is encouraged, this is a powerful tool.

---

### Figure 6.1—E-mail Guidelines for Format, Tone, Frequency, and Purpose

**Sources include:**

- E-mail netiquette guidelines from IEEE, **http://eleccomm.ieee.org/email-netiquette.shtml**

- "The Net: User Guidelines and Netiquette," by Arlene Rinaldi, Florida Atlantic University, **http://wise.fau.edu/netiquette/net/elec.html**

- " A Beginner's Guide to Effective E-mail," Revision 2.0 by Kaitlin Duck Sherwood, **http://www.webfoot.com/advice/email.top.html**

- Handouts available from the National Writing Center Association website: **http://nwca.syr.edu/NWCA/WCHandouts.html**

  In using e-mail as a tool for communicating with others within the context of a scheduled class, the following issues should be pointed out, discussed, and enforced.

**Format**— Design the way the reader of e-mail sees information. The goal of the e-mail format is readability and effective communication. Be clear and straightforward, avoiding unnecessary verbiage. If there is a longer message that needs to be communicated, consider creating this as a word processed document that can be attached to a brief e-mail message. An attached document should be in a standard word processing format such as Microsoft Word™ or the sender takes the risk that the document can not be read by the intended reader.

Begin the communication by providing identification— who is writing the message? Also include a descriptive subject header that gives the reader enough information that they can decide when and under what circumstances to open and read the e-mail. Remember that the first indication of the e-mail for the intended reader (typically) is as a listing of e-mail that only shows the sender name, the date received, and the subject of the e-mail. Many e-mail readers will examine this e-mail table of contents and decide what to read and what to throw away without reading, based on who is sending the information and what is noted in the subject heading.

**Tone**— Tone refers to the overall emotional content of the language used for the e-mail. While email often feels like a private communication, it is not. E-mail is a relatively public activity, semi-private at best. Don't write things that you would not be concerned about having others read. E-mail is easily forwarded, either by the recipient to others or by the sender, often by accident. This being said, there are a few cautions to note about what you write in an e-mail and how you write it. These include:

- *Avoid inflammatory language.* E-mail text is often written without the usual drafting process that might weed out wording or use of phrases that can anger someone else. It is easy to write something that others may misinterpret because the text is written quickly.

- *Misunderstandings also may occur* because the informality of e-mail text, written in haste, will not adequately convey the correct inflection and subtle shading of meaning intended. The rapidity of e-mail text suggests the informality of spoken communication but does not have the same cues for meaning.
- In responding to the e-mail of others, *be careful about quoting their e-mail, and about forwarding their e-mail to others. Taking wording out of context, especially the limited c*ontext of e-mail, can lead to major concerns by the people being quoted or by those receiving your e-mail.
- *Do not send e-mail using all uppercase (capital) letters or all lowercase letters.* Messages in uppercase are interpreted as shouting. In either situation, the readability of the message is damaged and the likelihood of misunderstandings is increased.

**Frequency and Purpose** — Note to instructors: In a class environment, attention should be paid to the pedagogical rationale for using e-mail with students. Often this includes a trade-off of important options: regularity of frequent contact and communication on the one hand and in-depth writing on the other. Be clear about how often you expect students to e-mail and for what purposes. It may be more important that students e-mail each other (possibly with copies to you) than sending too-frequent e-mails to the instructor. The best advice is to be clear about the expectations. A good rule of thumb is that students should communicate with the instructor a minimum of once per week for traditional classes—courses that meet in person one, two, or three times per week. For classes that meet less often or not at all in person, the contact should be increased, particularly if this is a primary mode of contact and connection between the instructor and the student.

## Presentation software

Presentation software affords instructors many options for demonstrating class materials and for classroom instructional options. The instructor can use presentation software, such as Microsoft PowerPoint™, as a didactic aid during lectures. They also can incorporate presentation projects by students, as individuals or teams, to encourage active learning. The power of presentation software lies in its ability to incorporate a wide variety of media—text, audio, video, charts, links to websites and database files. In this way supporting materials of almost unimaginable variety may be used during a presentation. A further element provided by presentation software is timing; all of the items presented—each "page" is referred to as a "slide"—may be given a specific time signature and automated or made dependent on some action, such as a mouse click, by the presenter.

A good model for using presentation software as an aid to improve instructional quality involves looking at various component steps of a class presentation:

Step (1) **Attention and motivation**—Begin the class by gaining the attention of the students and proceed by moving the focus of their attention to the subject matter of the class. Among the common strategies for this are using rhetorical questions, introducing an example from current events that has strong general interest, or presenting a visual metaphor—some instructors use a cartoon or humorous anecdote. Good practice in this step recognizes that the attention of any audience is rather fleeting; move quickly to make connections between getting their attention and the ideas, approaches, or materials for the class. Once the attention of the class is engaged, move to personalize the context of the class opener while connecting it to the subject of the class. Let your enthusiasm for what you are teaching show.

For this step, presentation software can provide a wide range of suitable tools for gaining the attention of students, including video clips of current news footage or an audio passage with accompanying text from a student presentation.

**Step (2) Overview**—Provide a general overview of what the class will be examining or discussing that day. This overview prepares the student and gives them a sense of how this material fits with what they already know. The overview includes a description of the various activities of the day's class, the broad topics, and a sense of what is expected of students—will they work in groups? Is there going to be a quiz at the end of class? Should they make sure they have their textbook at hand? The overview provides a road map for what is going to happen and helps to ensure that the students are prepared to meet expectations.

**Step (3) Content**—As the course material is offered to students, presentation software can help. Consider the kinds of content goals for the class.

- *Building a knowledge base.* The instructor presents information to students expecting that they are able to define, recall, identify, and remember. Building a basis for further work can be enhanced by additional reinforcing modes of media presentation. A good practice is providing this material, including the media presentation, to students on disk, via a website, or through an e-mail attachment.

- *Achieving a level of comprehension.* Students need to be able to paraphrase and summarize by explaining key concepts in their own words. A presentation slide can be used to cue this activity for the class as well as be used as a stimulator for student response.

- *Analyzing complex materials.* Student need to be able to

break down presented materials into their component parts, make inferences and categorize and draw conclusions based on evidence. The use of presentation software can foster this activity by being a focal point for displaying student work. As students demonstrate these skills, they can enter data and text and images that could be shown to the entire class for follow-up discussion.

- *Combining pieces into something new.* Students may be asked to take various elements of learned material and make predictions about what would come next, to be able to synthesize source materials or to rewrite and revise previous work in light of new or additional information. A good use of presentation software is asking students to create a class presentation that integrates a variety of material and demonstrates their ability to combine these into something new.

- *Assessing the quality of information.* Students need to be able to evaluate data, to appraise the value and relevance of particular elements to the class goals, to compare and contrast, and to come to some conclusions about the materials presented or discussed. Presentation software can be used to help pull source materials and critiques together for students to demonstrate their evaluative skills.

Step (4) **Summarize and reinforce**—This step is similar to the overview in that it presents a summary of presented content with a certain amount of "spin control", but it also reinforces the learning by letting students know what comes next. Connected to a repeat of the main points, this is the time to indicate what the students are expected to do with this information. Describe homework or other tasks that use the presented materials.

Note: this is *not* the time to introduce anything new; save it for the next class or a follow-up class e-mail. Use presentation software to show slides of key points and to make class assignments that follow-up and use the class materials.

Step (5) Close—An often ignored instructional step is making a definitive closing for the class. Make sure students know when the class is over. If students don't know what to expect—including when the class ends—they are likely to decide it is over at a different point than the instructor. An appropriately understood ending helps ensure that all students stay until the end. Some instructors use a closing story or cartoon while others close by offering specific announcements that are of common interest.

A common ending (not recommended) is finishing a class by asking if there are any questions and when none are forthcoming, declare the class over. This makes it unlikely that students will ask questions—who wants to be the only thing standing in the way of being able to leave the room at the end of a long class?

A better ending (recommended) is to use the last few minutes to ask students to write down one question or comment on the class that the instructor then collects. Once the student completes this task, they can exit the classroom. This kind of ending provides a trigger to leave based on completing a task. The important thing is to ensure that students have a reason to stay until the end and that the ending is clear and consistently done.

The instructor can use presentation software to have a definitive and distinctive ending that is consistently performed each class. A slide can cue the students to write a "one-minute paper," by giving one question or comment to discuss.

## Finding Information on the Internet

The rapid growth of data on the Internet has made finding something quickly and easily more challenging for the teacher and student. While there is a dizzying array of information available on virtually any topic, just try to find it. A simple search for a key word or name turns up far too many websites to be useful; "Martin Luther King," for example, recently returned nearly two million results. Among the results were websites related to a range of items including the holiday, memorial library, and speeches devoted to Martin Luther King. While it might be possible that the first few results listed are the pages sought, the greater likelihood is that the search will result in more frustration than desired information. Instructors can and should address this problem while helping students learn better ways for doing Web-based research.

> *As with other kinds of information searches, Web-based research follows the usual processes of search and find, evaluate and verify, followed by appropriate use and citation.*

One search strategy uses well-established sites that have collected information resources into a kind of data warehouse of other previewed websites. These core sites may be owned and maintained by non-profit educational institutions (often a university), non-profit organizations (**http://www.merlot.org**, for example) or for-profit corporations (such as **http://www.Bigchalk.com** ). One highly recommended site is the World Lecture Hall at the University of Texas: **http://www.utexas.edu/world/lecture/index.html**. As noted at their website, the "World Lecture Hall publishes links to pages created by faculty worldwide who are using the Web to deliver course materials in any language." A common feature of these warehouse sites is that they collect materials and websites, organize them into discrete categories and provide tools that enable users to locate resources within the site.

Another search strategy uses specialized search software or search engines. Whether proprietary or in the public domain, search engines try to find and index as many websites and Web pages as possible. Various search engines will boast about the number of sites in their indexing; others may claim an advantage based on their speed and search accuracy. The search indexing offered by the various search engines tends to be based on specific website characteristics, including unique key words, combinations of words, searching for particular fields of information, and limiting factors (boolean searches). No single search engine is able to index a very large portion of the World Wide Web, and none can find specific kinds of information that are behind some kind of entry portal (sites which require a searcher to log in). The content of specially formatted documents, such as Adobe™ PDF documents, is not searched even when the document itself is available on the Web. Understanding the features of several search engines will help students learn to use each for particular purposes.

The more common search engines include:

> *Google*—**www.google.com**—a large index that includes the websites of many organizations; fast; uses – and/or OR boolean operators; can limit search by language and domain.

> *Fast*—**www.alltheweb.com**—a very large index; among the fastest; uses some boolean operators; can limit search by language and domain; searches for multimedia.

> *Northern Light*—**www.northernlight.com**—a large and growing index with powerful search features; fee-based access to online publications; specialized search domains; free personalized news and research e-mail updates.

> *AltaVista*—**www.altavista.com**—a very large index with powerful and unique searching capabilities; boolean searching with extensive language search limits.

Beyond these few, there are many other search engines and more are becoming available. Students and faculty need to be familiar with the search tools most pertinent to their area of study. For additional information on Internet search engines, see the websites of Greg Notess, **http://www.notess.com**.

Exercises in searching for information can provide a fun and useful way for instructors to include Internet researching into the context of a class. Instructors can develop elementary levels of familiarity by using exercises that ask students to find a variety of kinds of information and websites—a Web scavenger hunt. Students can work in small teams or individually and can report back on their success at finding certain kinds of data. In addition to easily found responses, ("At which website would you be most likely to find information related to federal oversight of water quality?"), students can be asked to make qualitative choices as a part of this assignment, ("At which websites would you find the most useful information related to the disputes over water quality in the Rio Grande water basin?")

One good search practice limits the search to specified URL domains. In this way the student can have some greater confidence that the material on population statistics, for example, from a website with the URL <.gov>, is probably reliable and based on governmental census data. Good practice extends the exercise of research skill from search to a level that asks students to make decisions about the quality of the information received.

Evaluating the quality of information and verifying the accuracy of the materials on the Web represents a major issue for teaching using the Web. Even if students can find information, the real question is whether the information is useful and/or valid. Anyone can put information out on the Web—and usually does; there is no requirement that it be validated in the same way information published in a reviewed journal. One-way to address this is to use sites that are reviewed, such as sites of major academic journals or full-text databases of various journals. These are often not searched when general purpose search engines look at the Web; for these the student may need to use the proprietary tools of the campus library or state library system.

Four criteria for evaluating Web pages and the information listed there, includes:

- **Who is the author?** Check the accuracy of Web documents by making sure that a name and affiliation is listed. Is there an e-mail address listed that can be used to follow up on the information? Is this person qualified to provide the information on the website? Why was this website created? Does it have an educational or commercial function?

- **What are the credentials of the author?** What is the authority of the website? What is the URL domain? Is the domain from an educational institution (.edu), governmental entity (.gov), organizational group (.org), or business (.com/.biz)? Are there citations for the data presented?

- **How objective is the material presented?** Try to determine if there is a hidden agenda or commercial purpose to the information. Ask why and for whom the Web page was created. One clue could be the detail of the information. What kinds of sources are cited for the data presented?

- **How current and up-to-date is the information presented?** Find out when the document was created or when it was last updated. Are there any dead links on the page? If so, this is a clue that the page has not changed recently and might indicate that the information on the page is outdated.

Additional websites that are useful when searching for information:

http://brainblitz.com Enables user to watch other searches on the Web. See how others search and what kinds of information is being searched.

http://unige.ch/meta-index.html W3 Search Engines; collection of many search engines and tools for finding information on the Web.

http://whyfiles.org The Why Files; the science behind the news.

http://edsitement.neh.fed.us Edsitement; National Endowment for the Humanities on the Web; many source materials available from this site.

http://www.researchpaper.com Source of topics and ideas for student research.

http://www.loc.gov Library of Congress homepage; key site for governmental data.

http://thomas.loc.gov Legislative information on the Internet.

http://www.emtech.net/learning_styles.html Bibliography and collection of URLs related to learning styles.

http://www.lib.uiowa.edu/proj/Webbuilder/copyright.html Copyright and multimedia legal issues for website creators and authors.

http://www.du.org/cybercomp.html Composition in cyberspace; key source for information on writing and the Internet.

The appropriate use of Web information is specific to the course of study and the particular instructor (keyed to pedagogy). What is important here is that the instructor incorporate the use of search techniques with the class, instruct students in evaluation and verification of the information contained in the websites, and finally, ensure that students appropriately cite any information found on the Web.

# References

Angelo T. & Cross K. (1993). *Classroom assessment techniques: A handbook for college teachers* (2nd ed.). San Francisco: Jossey-Bass.

Bianco-Mathis, V. et al. (1996). *The adjunct faculty handbook.* Thousand Oaks, CA: Sage Publications, Inc.

Bloom, B. et. al. (1956). *Taxonomy of educational objectives.* New York: David McKay.

Burnstad, H. (2000). Developing the environment for learning. In Greive D, (ed.). *Handbook II-Advanced teaching strategies for adjunct and part-time faculty.* Elyria. OH: Info-Tec.

Chickering, A. & Ehrmann, S. (1997). Seven principles for good practice in undergraduate education. *American Association for Higher Education Bulletin, 3-87.*

Greive, D. (Ed.). (2000). *Handbook II-Advanced teaching strategies for adjunct and part-time faculty.* Elyria OH: Info-Tec.

Knowles, M. (1990). *The adult learner-A neglected species.* Houston, TX: Gulf Publishing.

Mager, R. (1962). *Preparing instructional objectives.* Belmont, CA: Fearon Publishers.

McCarthy, B. (1987). *The 4-MAT system.* Barrington, IL: Excel, Inc.

McKeachie, W. et. al. (1994). *Teaching tips, strategies, research and theory for college and university teachers.* Lexington, MA: D. C. Heath and Co.

NEA, (1975). <www.new.org/aboutnea/code.html.>

Sego, A. (1994). *Cooperative learning-A classroom guide.* Elyria, OH: Info-Tec.

Salmon, J. (1994). The diverse classroom. In Frye, B. (ed). *Teaching in college-A resource for college teachers.* Elyria OH: Info-Tec.

Stephan, K., (2000). The syllabus and the lesson plan. In Greive, D. (ed). *Handbook II-Advanced teaching strategies for adjunct and part-time faculty.* Elyria, OH: Info-Tec.

Weimer, M. *Improving college teaching.* San Francisco: Jossey-Bass.

# Index

## A

academic dishonesty 25
accountability 9, 68, 94
active learning 36, 48, 82, 99, 100, 102, 110
affective domain 37
*AltaVista* (Search Engine) 115
andragogy 32
anecdotes 10, 13, 16, 18-21, 36, 38, 46, 68, 74-76, 89, 110
Angelo, T.A. 48
AOL (Internet Service Provider) 104

## B

barriers 15, 37, 40, 42, 45
bell curve 30, 95
Bianco-Mathis, V. 65
Bloom, Benjamin 37
Bloom's Taxonomy of Educational Objectives 37, 49, 58
bulletin board, computer 89
Burnstad, Helen 11
buzz groups 19, 86, 88

## C

case studies 87, 102
chatroom, computer 89
cheating 25
Chickering, Art 97
chronological outline 59
class expert (student type) 46
classroom assessment 13, 29, 48, 49, 65
classroom behavior 46, 52
classroom evaluation 52
classroom research 48
classroom styles 85
Code of Ethics of the Education Profession 24
cognitive domain 37
cognitive learners 35
collaborative learning 19, 33, 39, 83, 88, 99
college policies 65
community-centered learning 11
computer-based tutoring 100

# K

Knowles, Malcolm 32

# L

laissez-faire classroom 20, 42
large group instruction 80, 88, 89
learning cells 85
learning college 11
learning hierarchy 92
learning styles 20, 34, 35, 102, 103, 117
lecture 36, 49, 71, 73-76, 81, 83, 85, 88-91, 99, 102
legal issues 23, 55
lesson plans 33, 55, 60, 68
listservs 89, 105

# M

Mager, Robert 58
Maslow, Abraham 39
Maslow's Hierarchy of Needs 39
McCarthy, B. 34
McKeachie, Wilbert 22
media, influences of 30
Microsoft PowerPoint 110
Microsoft Word 108
minute paper 48
motivation 38
muddiest point 49
multimedia 68, 71, 72, 90, 110-117
multiple choice 93
multiple-choice 92, 93

# N

National Education Association 24
negative student (student type) 47
netiquette 107
networks 97, 104
non-verbal communication 41, 83
Northern Light (Search Engine) 115
Notess, Greg 115

# O

# P

# Q

# R

# S

| If you found this book helpful, you'll want to check out these other titles: |
|---|

### Handbook II: Advanced Strategies for Adjunct and Part-time Faculty by Donald Greive

*Handbook II* carries on the tradition of practical and readable instructional guides that began with *A Handbook for Adjunct & Part-time Faculty* (new in a fourth edition!)

Intended for adjuncts who have already mastered the basics and for the managers of adjunct faculty, *Handbook II* offers in-depth coverage of some of the topics you just read about like andragogy, collaborative learning, syllabus construction, and testing. But this manual also goes beyond these topics to discuss specific teaching techniques for critical thinking, problem solving, large class instruction and distance learning assignments.

Brand-new in November, 2000, *Handbook II* gives you expert and current strategies to take your teaching to the next level. Available in paperback for $16.00 each.

---

### Managing Adjunct & Part-time Faculty in the New Millennium edited by Donald Greive and Catherine Worden

New and exciting changes are taking place in higher education every day and one of the many tasks of an adjunct faculty manager is to keep up with these changes and communicate them back to their adjunct and part-time faculty.

In *Managing Adjunct & Part-time Faculty in the New Millennium,* noted author and educator Donald Greive has collected works from many experts in their fields. discussing topics like institutional quality, ethical and legal issues, faculty development, and distance education technology--all in a single volume.

Also new for 2000, *Managing Adjunct & Part-time Faculty* is available in hardcover for $34.95 and in paperback for $24.95.

---

# FAQ's...

## How can I place an orders?

Orders can be placed **by mail** to The Adjunct Advocate, P.O. Box 130117, Ann Arbor, MI 48113-0117, **by phone** at (734)930-6854, **by fax** at (208)728-3033, and **via the Internet** at http://www.AdjunctNation.com and select Bookstore to be taken to the secure Web site.

## How much do I pay if I want multiple copies?

Each of the Adjunct Advocate, Inc. products has a quantity discount schedule available. The schedule for the new *Handbook* is:

**1-9 copies**--$15.00 each     **10-49 copies**--$7.50 each
**50-99 copies**--$6.75 each   **100 or more copies**--$5.25 each

## How can I pay for orders?

Orders can be placed on **a purchase order** or can be paid by **check** or **credit card** (Visa/Mastercard, Discover or AMEX.)

## How will my order be shipped?

Standard shipping to a continental U.S. street address is via **UPS-Ground Service**. Foreign shipments or U.S. post office box addresses go through the **U.S. Postal Service** and express shipments via **UPS-2nd Day, UPS-Next Day**, or **Fedex**. Shipping and handling charges are based on the dollar amount of the shipment, and a fee schedule is shown on the next page.

## What if I'm a reseller like a bookstore or wholesaler?

Resellers get a standard **20 percent discount** off of the single copy retail price. This discount structure allows resellers a **three-month return** period from the date of invoicing.

## Adjunct Advocate, Inc.  Instructional Products

| Qty | Author:Title | Unit $$ | Total |
|---|---|---|---|
| | Handbook for Adjunct/Part-Time Faculty | (pb) $15.00 | |
| | Handbook II | (paperback) $16.00 | |
| | Adjunct Professor's Guide to Success | (paperback) $35.00 | |
| | Managing Adjunct/Part-Time Faculty | (paperback) $24.95 | |
| | Teaching Strategies and Techniques | (paperback) $10.95 | |
| | Teaching Tips | (paperback) $35.00 | |
| | How to Survive as an Adjunct Lecturer | (paperback) $17.95 | |
| | The Online Teaching Guide | (paperback) $38.00 | |
| | Academic Job Search Handbook | (paperback )$16.00 | |
| | Quick Hits: Award-winning Teaching Strategies | (paperback $12.95 | |
| | *Adjunct Advocate*: A Journal for Adjunct/Part-time, Visiting and Full-Time Temporary Faculty (**Single 1-yr. subscription**)  $35.00 | | |
| | | **Subtotal** | |
| | | **Shipping & Handling (See below)** | |
| | | **Total** | |
| | **Purchaser/Payment Information** | | |

☐   Check (payable to The Adjunct Advocate)
☐   Credit Card # _____ Exp. Date _____
☐   Purchase Order # _____

Name _____ Title_____
Institution_____
Address _____ City/ST/Zip_____
Phone: _____ FAX:_____ E-mail:_____

## Shipping and Handling Fee Schedule:

| | |
|---|---|
| $0-$30 purchase | $5.00 |
| $31-$75 purchase | $10.00 |
| Purchases over $75 | 7% of purchase subtotal |